Strings of Life, Fate & Hope

Written by:

LIZ CHORNEY
Nee (Smolinski)

Order this book online at www.trafford.com
or email orders@trafford.com

Most Trafford titles are also available at major online book retailers.

Print information available on the last page.

ISBN: 978-1-4120-5911-4 (sc)
ISBN: 978-1-4122-3636-2 (e)

Trafford rev. 11/09/2022

North America & international
toll-free: 844-688-6899 (USA & Canada)
fax: 812 355 4082

Strings of Life, Fate & Hope

Written by:

LIZ CHORNEY
Nee (Smolinski)

Introduction

This story follows the life of an early pioneer immigrant who is called to North America in the year1900. More specifically, it is a chronicle of my Baba's or my Grandmother's life, and the driving force that brought sustenance, direction, and hope, in the most trying times. May you who read this story reflect upon the life of your own ancestors and rediscover the mark that those before us left behind as their legacy, celebrating life along and life's uncertainties, while building families, communities, and a nation!

In the years prior to 1900, Canadian agents were milling about Europe promoting the beauty of Canada's vistas and the splendid future that awaited those who would relocate to a new country! These agents were also promising free homesteads. Free homesteads to anyone wishing to undertake the adventure of breaking land into arable fields made ripe for sowing! Prime emigrants for entrance consideration are; young families, strong able-bodied men, as well as adventurous women! More specifically unattached single women, those willing to function in the role of someone's domestic help or spouse, as, in Canada, there are countless men longing for the companionship of a female helper or mate!

My Baba, determinedly sought that brighter future in a new country when she repeatedly heard, 'a beckoning reassuring voice'. Thus, at the tender age of fourteen, she left behind her family, her home, and her childhood acquaintances in a Selo, or small village; named Pidkamin, near the town of Brody, in the Oblast (region) of Lviv; at which time in history belonged to the principality or ruling state of Austria!

On her arrival to Halifax, Canada, she mustered the energy to board a train and make her way to the province of Manitoba. In the city of Winnipeg, she fortunately connected to friends from her village. These acquaintances were instrumental in securing her first job placement in the field of her proficiency, documented by immigration as that of a domestic helper!

After two long years of tending to other people's needs, my Baba was ready for a new adventure. A governmental 'promised free homestead' to any immigrant, definitely sounded intriguing when presented by a proposing future spouse. Geared up to forge a life as a self-reliant pioneer homesteader, she heads off to a newly established rural community called Ladywood, located in the recently formed Municipality of Brokenhead, Manitoba, Canada.

As a typical pioneer on that 'promised free homestead,' my Baba was, without a doubt, predestined to a lifetime of endless struggle and labour! Periodically, alone on the 160 acres of inhospitable surroundings, she would work hard to make a life for her offspring to survive.

But; the most remarkable fact is, that at no time did the taxing work, to convert swamp, dense forest, and stone into a ready field; give my Baba reason to lose hope on that legislated 'Gratis Land Site,' located east of the Prime Meridian, on the northeast quarter of Section 22, Township 14 and Range 7. At this location, the better life she sought for herself and her progeny was with time, to unfold.

Note To The Reader

Within the story are a number of Ukrainian words or phrases. (Bold type) These inserts will be followed in turn, by a close literal translation in the English language text. These Ukrainian phrases or words are phonetically pronounced using the English alphabetic sounds rather than the Cyrillic alphabetic sounds; therefore, the exact or refined pronunciation may somewhat fall short in the correct and polished pronunciation!

A key to aid you in the pronunciation of all-Ukrainian words!

A or **a** - as in f**a**r

E or **e** - as in g**e**t

EE or **ee** - as in f**ee**t

Y or **y** - as 'y' in s**y**mbol,
   if **Y** or **y** are followed by a vowel
   then pronounce with vowel sound,
   as given below!

   YE or **ye** - as in **ye**s

   YEE or **yee** - as the "yea" in **yea**st

   YU or **yu** - as "yu" in **yu**le

   YA or **ya** - as in **YA**LTA

O or **o** - as in **o**r

U or **u** - as in d**u**plicate

KH or **kh** - as the "ch" in Ba**ch**
   or Scottish lo**ch**

ZH or **zh** - as the "s" in vi**s**ion

TS or **ts** - as in Pat**s**y

SH or **sh** - as in **sh**ot

SHCH or **shch** - as fre**sh ch**eese

Other bold type inserts are songs minus the musical score.

vii

Secondary Key to Pronunciation

A or *a* - as in f*a*r

E or *e* - as in g*e*t

EE or *ee* - as in f*ee*t

Y or *y* – as '*y*' in s*y*mbol,
    if **Y** or **y** are followed by a vowel
    then pronounce with vowel sound,
    as given below!

        YE or *ye* – as in *ye*s

        YEE or *yee* - as the "*yea*" in *yea*st

        YU or *yu* - as "*yu*" in *yu*le

        YA or *ya* - as in *YA*LTA

O or *o* - as in *o*r

U or *u* - as in d*u*plicate

KH or *kh* - as the "*ch*" in Ba*ch*
        or Scottish lo*ch*

ZH or *zh* - as the "*s*" in vi*s*ion

TS or *ts* - as in Pa*ts*y

SH or *sh* - as in *sh*ot

SHCH or *shch* - as fre*sh ch*eese

Acknowledgements

This testimonial of appreciation to the life of my grandmother was mostly based on factual information provided by my dear Uncle Stanley Smolinski, to whom I am most grateful. Also, many Thanks to my Ukrainian friends who encouraged me so immensely while I strived to re-learn the Ukrainian language as an adult, and who, so willingly helped me with some of the translations for this story! More so, I will always be indebted to my family, friends, and many new acquaintances that so amiably took an active part as my mentors, to all a big Thank-You!

Lastly, had my life been as challenging as that of my early ancestors, or had I not the opportunity to receive a reasonable education, the means to afford a computer as well as the resources to invest in electronic publishing; this story would have more than likely gone undocumented and definitely unpublished.

LIZ

A Voice That Called

Periodically, it is good to take the time to pay tribute to those who listened to that inner guiding voice. A voice, which in some way called each new immigrant, to pack up all of his or her belongings, relinquish the life that he or she knew, and journey to this foreign country called Canada! If it were not for those who came before us with an inward reassurance of their dreams and visions, that another place could bring more hope, and bravely persevered when all seemed but hopeless, probably ninety percent of us would not be here to enjoy this life that was bought and paid for through all their sacrifices!

I am grateful to my ancestors who listened to that encouraging voice. A voice that directed them from the bondage of serfdom, to a life of autonomy within a community of embracing neighours, who, too; were led by that same inner voice of hope! I believe, that same phenomenal voice continues to call each and every one of us to this very day, in love, in honour and respect of all our diverse neighbours, as we continue to evolve and build the esteemed multicultural nation we are today. Led by this voice, we've blossomed into a nation that consists of hundreds of very diverse cultures and ethnicities, most of whom have learned to live in reasonable harmony, expressing different points of view, different faiths, different traditions and cultures, without the fear of reprisal! Today, this unity has labeled us with the global reputation of being, 'the envy of the world!' At the start of our nationhood, what key factors prevailed to make us the nation we are today? In pursuit of a few possible answers, I now invite you to come along with me on a journey to yesterday. The journey I wish to take you on is not an exotic one, but rather, one filled with many universal experiences shared by our pioneer ancestors, more than some one hundred years ago!

This narrative will be conveyed in a timed rhythm, or poetry and song. In bygone days, songs were used by most cultures to celebrate life's happiest moments as well as deal with life's trials and tribulations! Long before mood altering drugs or psychotherapies were made available for the benefit of one's mental health, songs were commonly used by our ancestors to express their lonesomeness and melancholy, their anxieties and fears, as well as their untold despairs and sorrows. In times past, it was all rather common for one to boldly chant, or sing, till peace had no choice but to enter into one's disheartened soul!

Obviously, music and song seemed to have a wonderful therapeutic effect for our ancestors. Their love of music played a vital part in banishing the distresses in life that, otherwise; would have troubled their heart or spirit to the point of suicidal ideation, had they not ousted these negative feelings through the merriment of song, and dance. I hope at the conclusion of this story, you too, will be singing and dancing your cares and worries away, and empowered to banish the cares and worries of others! So sit back and enjoy the story, which I bequeath to the life of all our Canadian ancestors who were, and to the life of all the generations of children, still to come!

This story is dedicated

TO LIFE;

Honouring

The life of our ancestors who were,

The life of their children,

The life of their children's children

And the life of those yet to come!

LIFE

To those who celebrate family!

LIFE,

To those who celebrate friends and neighbours!

LIFE

To those who celebrate the world around us!

LIFE,

To those who celebrate the power

That daily leads and guides us!

TO LIFE!

Strings of Life, Fate and Hope

Part One

This picture depicts only a small portion of the perimeter base of the Taras Shevchenko Memorial Monument, located on east side of the Manitoba Legislative grounds. On this base are castings of people in various occupations from another era, the center most casting is one of a Bandurist. A more complete monument picture to follow later.

Monument by Andry Daragan
Modern Art Foundry
New York N.Y. U.S.A

My Bandura awaits its completion. Components assembled and carved to date are; solid maple neck, to support the taunt base strings, center hollowed to provide a deep, rich resonance. The wheat carved cherry wood will cover the hollowed neck. The front of the Bandura is made with laminated Sitka spruce and cherry wood inserts. The back of the Bandura is wide bowl shaped and is made by laminating many pieces of a mahogany, the center is hollowed as well.

Birth of a Bandura and a Bandurist

Play bandura play, sing and tell …
How our people here did come,
Who was it who embraced them?
How our people here did come,
Who was it who embraced them?

Play bandura play, sing and tell …
How our people here did come,
Who was it who helped them?
How our people here did come,
Who was it who helped them?

While I was busy cutting, carving, gluing, and sanding pieces of wood to make the structural part of my Bandura, that song repeatedly came to my mind! This instrument would soon be finished, and I could help it tell the story. Except; not only would the necessary components be needed to complete my project, but also needed would be a good dose of some magical power. Some supernatural force, for that total transformation into one authentic Bandurist! In the not so distant past, just before the printed word became available to all of society; a typical Bandurist used this instrument as an adjunct in the presentation of many a true story or tale.

*It is documented that; for several centuries, all newsworthy events were relayed from one village to the next by wandering Bandurists or minstrels! These spoken word artists kept many a villager informed of the latest news happenings through their performances of mini-musical dramas, all done in timed rhythm, or poetry and song. They became renowned for their longer poem or story recitals, better known as '**du-my**', which recapitulated the epic deeds and actions of a deceased individual! Throughout the ages, these legendary Bandurists kept the recollections of remarkable people alive, till one day, both the Bandura and the Bandurist, were pointlessly silenced.*

*There are many '**du-my**' or stories of unsung heroes from our more recent past that demand telling, definitely without the fear of being hushed! If I was to play a part in this mission, my Bandura should best be assembled for authenticity sake! For the much needed supplies, I carried out an exhaustive search on the Internet. Getting no where fast in making my instrument playable, I began to muse over the possibility of connecting to the land and origin of this instrument's technology and the factory that, for years, manufactured this unusual mobile piano, with its sixty plus strings strung vertically over a carved body, shaped like an over-sized guitar.*

Before I knew it, I was planning a trip to Ukraine, for surely; there, I would find all the necessary hardware to complete my Bandura! Ukraine, also happened to be the birthplace of all my ancestors, and thus, it quickly became somewhat of a priority to do some fact-finding regarding the village and the life of my dear paternal Baba, or Granny! I always felt very close to this one particular Baba. But; oddly, I knew very little of my Baba's life either prior to, or after her arrival to Canada, which unquestionably shaped the person she became.

As a child, all I knew was that I liked my Baba totally. I liked her best when she'd present me with hard round peppermints, or maybe a quarter or two, an unexpected sum for the few cleaning jobs I carried out on my visits to her house on a Saturday. In due course, I knew the signs of her gratefulness. If she began to fish deep inside her bosom to locate her red and white polka dotted hanky, I would, without a doubt, hit pay dirt! The most excruciating aspect of this whole ordeal was watching her arthritic fingers trying to untie and retie the corner of the hanky that so securely stored her stash of coins. Her fumbling fingers mesmerized me. After she presented me with a coin or two, she carefully tallied the remains and then tightly re-knotted the square. With a few taxing folds, the handkerchief was transformed into a neat package. This treasure she discreetly placed back into her cleavage for safekeeping.

I also remember that on my visits, my Baba would evenly split a bottle drink and offer me rather artificial looking bought bread, all to energize me for my long two and a half-mile walk home! I watched her as she gently kissed her slice of fluffy white bread three times. The rest of our snack time could best be described as, totally uneventful! Just the two of us, chewing and drinking somewhat silently! This silence was not a continuation of reverence to the sharing of bread, but rather, created by a language barrier! Ukrainian was my mother tongue, my first spoken language, and I understood it well. Still, there was a point in my life that speaking this language became both an unbearable challenge and frustration. This inability to speak Ukrainian occurred as a result of various early childhood anguishes that so bunged the possibility of fully conversing with my Baba forever!

I wished that as a child I had rehearsed a few simple questions to query my Baba about her life, because as an adult, I was time after time, drawn to tell my Baba's story. A story for future generations to reacquaint themselves with the early life of our pioneer ancestors. If only I knew the whole saga! Still, from the very hallows of my half-completed string-less Bandura; words flowed mystically onto these crisp white pages, in a timed or metered rhythm, recorded for perpetuity, as an everlasting remembrance of not only my Baba's life but also the life of all other early immigrants!

Reminiscing

Certain memories of my Baba flow endlessly and replay in my mind.

So life-like are the scenes, occurring as if yesterday;

all happening in her cozy kitchen,

near the wood stove, where we tried to keep toasty warm.

There we shared many a bubbling, tingling pop,

along with slices of angelic-like white bread…

oddly in silence, the two of us, so often, just merely sat.

This was so ritualistic; it could best be described as norm.

But, it was in that kitchen,

where mounting tension would swell within me…

as next to that cook stove,

we'd make the customary attempt to have our usual chat!

The typical sort of talk between a grandma and a child,

still, it was a rather grueling experience.

A taxing routine indeed, for she simply spoke no English,

or maybe she would so deliberately let on,

having a child beside her, she'd try to relive her youth…

that was so swiftly swept, and long time gone!

I fully understood her whenever she would speak to me…

but how I laboured,

laboured to find the most suitable words,

the most appropriate words to answer her, Oh Gee!

I think, that this unusual predicament occurred

the moment that I had first started school.

Back then, only Ukrainian did I know

and very soon thereafter, a mental block developed,

when from a certain teacher came a swift strapping

or to the head a severe blow! Whack, went the thirty-six inch slim rule,

all for speaking a foreign language, when English was now the status quo!

There were also taunting and derogatory remarks that ensued day after day.

Dumb Bo Hunk, Galician, D.P.; short form for displaced person by the way.

These were only a few of the choice names

some thoughtless and cruel kids would repeatedly say,

trying to bully and upset me,

while on recess we were released to the great outdoors,

for supposedly, fifteen minutes of rollicking fun and play!

On any given day, this happened to be the longest fifteen minutes of my life.

If this was all to be a joke,

why were those bullying classmate's jokes not funny any more?

And why to others was my inability to speak English

becoming for them, such a piercing caustic thorn,

ending in a stream of name-calling that 'my being,' seemed to provoke.

Experiencing such physical and mental trauma,

being Ukrainian was definitely no fun!

So as to quickly 'fit in' and subdue the unwanted scorn,

and maybe a small portion of my emotional pain,

I had no choice, but to eject from my brain, the language of my roots,

with the hope of stopping the ridicule and disdain!

As a result this action,

exchanging any words with my Baba became an unbearable torment,

requiring that I frequently dodge her unending stream of questions,

over and over again, so as not to be outdone!

Distressed and restless, I continued to sit rather close to my Baba…

rocking madly back and forth, back and forth, in her rocking chair so fine.

All awhile; I was silently praying, she not ask so many complex questions…

trusting that my petitions would save me from bolting, and to the forest run!

For, her queries literally brought sweat to my brow,

as my mind worked double-time, trying to translate and decode

Ukrainian to English, then English to Ukrainian, as best as I knew how!

More often than not, I wasn't sure what to say, and would pathetically respond

with a shake of my head, up and down, side to side,

hoping to quickly conclude this query episode.

One incident from my childhood

I'll remember until my dying day,

I was wearing a certain outfit

when in Ukrainian she did so gently say.

"TO DE VY DEE-STA-LY" *(So where did you get that?)*

"SKEEL-KO KOSH-TU-VA-LO" *(How much did it cost?)*

Now, for lack of vocabulary,

the right words eluded my mind and I was completely lost!

As the clothing I wore, was neither to big, nor to small,

and probably to her failing eyes appeared new to her,

but sadly it was… none other than, a well fitting hand-me-down!

Struggling to think of the most fitting and correct words to answer her,

I promptly knew… that, we were fast approaching,

a very severe, communication breakdown!

Hand-me-down! Hand-me-down! Hand-me-down!

At this point I recognized, I had to keep all her questioning at bay

and somehow evade explaining that which I knew,

I hadn't the foggiest idea, as to how those three words to say.

As I grew more anxious,

the devil within had shown his sway

thereby so cleverly assisting me,

with the telling of this little white lie.

"How my Mother and Father took me shopping,

shopping…

to an unbelievable big store in Winnipeg called EATON'S, *

Eaton's Bargain Basement;

and it was there that, this new outfit…

we just happened to buy!"

Well,

my Baba then took it upon herself to ask the price of everything I wore

and I became absolutely dumbfounded,

when she wanted to know more…of all the merchandise

I might have seen on display, within that huge department store!

Of course, 'THAT PLACE,' I only heard a lot about,

living far out in the country,

I had not been so privileged to visit the big city yet!

In an effort to save face, do I fabricate another story?

And if so, what now should I say to appropriately describe it?

Deep in thought,

formulating, and reformulating, the most suitable reply,

my anxiety soared, rocking back forth in a motion more quickened.

There I was, gaining such speed and momentum,

from that chair I thought, I could fully fly!

In all probability… I could have been sky riding,

had I not turned down her 'gas forming' bean and sauerkraut soup!

Unexpectedly, a huge tear I spotted, that rolled so ever slowly…

down the corner of my Baba's wrinkled lined eye,

as she sat close beside me, in her rather usual hunched stoop.

At that precise moment, I wished we could truly fly…

for I so wanted to grasp my Baba's frail, pale hand

and away we'd skyrocket together

to a never-ending, "Shopping Land!"

As I was more than certain,

that in her heart, she must have longed…

to shop downtown in a fashionable grand store,

but shopping was totally beyond her, and shopping she did no more.

Given, that at about the same time I got to know my Baba,

a form of crippling and disabling arthritis had by then…

made all her walking attempts, extremely difficult and sore.

However,

she remained so inquisitive of the world that daily beckoned…

just beyond the two rows of heavenly smelling lilacs,

that so graced and sheltered the welcoming entrance

of her country home's front door!

To her many questions,

*I usually replied, in a quick…***"Ya ne-zna-yoo!"***

In English, "I don't know!"

But, did my Baba really buy that malarkey?

Or did she know…that this was far from being so?

I know now, she knew more then she would really let on,

in days of her bold, harsh youth…long, long time gone!

Nonetheless, so little did I know of my Baba,

till I was surprisingly enlightened

by some of the many recollections of my Uncle, her son!

I told my Uncle of my intention to trek back to the land of my ancestral roots

as something was steadily driving me to connect to the place of my Baba's birth.

Since, maybe in reality, this dream was going to happen at last,

he and I needed to reminisce on old memoirs that could disclose, or unearth…

the sequence and the life,

of his mothers hardly ever heard-of past!

"My mother's maiden name was **Ma-ry-na** *or Mary Wyhrysta. In 1900 at*

the age of fourteen she emigrated from a small village in Brody, Austria.

Previously it was Poland, later occupied by Germany and then the Soviet

Union; currently it is now Ukraine. Here it is on the map! Boy oh boy;

if you go there, look for anyone having Wyhrysta as his or her last name

and find out if maybe we could be related! Spelled **W-y-h-r-y-s-t-a**, *I think*

that's how it was spelt, or maybe it was **V-y-h-r-y-s-t-a**. *The immigration*

officials would write the names down the way they heard them. Sometimes,

you know; they would spell them so funny, and so terribly incorrect!"

Footnote: *Old documents show her name spelled as Maria Wychrysta*

As my Uncle started to tell me his mother's life story,

I suddenly noticed,

now that he was older,

his persona so reminded me of her

and, for some strange reason,

his voice trailed off and her voice came in…

expressing a weight of emotions, astonishingly in English!

As a matter of fact, wonderful English, and in poetic verse as well!

Was I sitting in the same galactic space,

or did my Baba invade mine?

This occurrence baffled me, along with her near perfect speech!

Was she or was she not illiterate in the English language,

or was that a game she played

so that the language of my roots would never be forgotten

and always be maintained?

When I asked my uncle about his mother's English literacy skills,

his final thoughts were… she knew more than she would let on,

but for some unknown reason she kept it all very much restrained!

Footnote:

*EATON'S was one of the biggest departmental stores in Winnipeg from 1905-1999, selling a full array of merchandise, namely…dry goods, clothing, furniture, appliances, and hardware. There was a time, when Eaton's subsidiary, the Eaton's Catalogue, sold, in addition to the above, ready to assemble homes. These homes were cost effective and less time consuming for the newly arrived settlers to build, both of which were important in quickly fulfilling their housing needs. The Catalogue used the postal services to deliver their goods to the rural buying public. Winnipeg residents received home delivery, firstly by horse and wagon, as motorized vehicles came on the scene; these became more advantageous for deliveries. Eaton's Bargain Basement was located in the main eight-storey complex and was the lowest level. The basement was definitely the place that an astute shopper would not miss out on, as it was there one would find the best value priced items.

Baba's Haunting Words

In my mind's eye, my Baba came to life as my Uncle spoke.

Larger in existence than I ever knew her to be!

Yet, rather than question this strange phenomenon,

I allowed this force to take over the role of my Uncle, the interviewee.

And strangely, without hesitation, my Baba did speak…

"I will tell all,

to those who care to listen, or to those who care know…

of my adventurous or not so adventurous life,

that happened to me, so many eons and eons ago!

I was such a very young girl…

when someone repeatedly spoke to my heart,

persistently encouraging me with my immediate family,

as well as my dear Ukraine, to forever part!

This stirring voice quickly rid all doubts from my mind,

but sharing any of it with my family and friends,

now that was just a matter of a much different kind!

These intimate messages crept deep into my dreams at night,

rousing my thoughts by day with scores of new daydreams.

At first I did wonder… whether I could be completely all right!

But nightly three words repeatedly echoed loud and clear…

"Do not fear! Do not fear! DO NOT FEAR!"

Words that brought such joy and exhilaration on each new waking day,

that; I couldn't stop myself from blurting out saying…

"God will look after me," attempting to dispel the fears of all,

when friends and family disapprovingly, would have these few words to say.

Vy ta-kee mo-lo-dee, *("You are so young,)*

Yak vy-tam ye-de-te, *(How can you go,)*

Do mee-sto sho vy ne-zna-ye-te?

(To a city what you do not know?")

In the hope of leaving behind oppression and adversity

created by serfdom*, as well as repeated conflict and war,

I held fast to two vital prerequisites. My bribed false passport,

readily obtained by some baby-faced street kid, who…

occasionally came begging to our family's front door!

So splendidly was this passport altered,

shifting my birth backwards by a whole two years

and thereby magically making me, 'Sweet Sixteen Years Of Age!'

A two-year difference, changed by a fine nib of a pen, with complete ease!

*Serfdom – A serf or slave labourer held in bondage of servitude to the feudal landowner.

Then there was my ticket all paid for,

with my own blood, sweat, and many sobbing tears,

while I laboured at a hilltop monastery as a domestic,

*under the barking directions of a **PAN**! ***

A man elevated above others, like a lord,

but being near him, in terror, I'd shudder and freeze!

Well how could I best say it?

He was a real low down intolerant person…

breathing down on the necks of us young inexperienced peasant girls

in lashing, despicable and frightful fits of rage!

From the age of nine I worked in that huge castle,

when really I should have been at school…

instead, there I daily scrubbed miles of brick floor,

blistering my baby soft hands and knees.

The money I earned went to my parents, however,

some I slyly put aside for my passage,

hoping that with the coming of my adulthood

I'd have the means to start life on a brand new page

and finally do exactly… what I darn well please!

Given that; at an early age, somehow I knew...

that if one's life was trapped into peasantry,

it invariably brought impoverishment as well as shame and scorn!

Having no choice as to the fate of who my proud parents might be,

it was my fortune that, into a peasant family, I happened to be born!

Under control of the estate holder or Pan,

who incidentally were always rich and powerful,

life for our family became a test at survival!

One's belly was never full and hunger became a well-known trend.

As peasant landowners we were increasingly taxed to the hilt,

and over time, it was ever more difficult to meet the escalating levying demand...

of either money or grain.

These assets were to be turned over on time to the Pan

as the set standard rule!

The end result of serfdom was the ongoing insult of hunger and poverty,

created heartlessly by the Pan, the church, and the monarchy, all for their gain...

to extort cheap labour from the inhabitants, over whom they did reign!

For, we peasants were bound to them alone,

as a result of our tenure, on a small plot of land!

Irrelevant of our age or health,

each and everyone was required to go,

and contribute our labours

towards the betterment of our master's domain!

There in the fields we'd bend with a sickle in hand,

moving as fast as we could,

to and fro…

in type of a rhythmic dance to a shouted upbeat lilt,

labouring till in pain…

for a meager pittance,

and maybe an armful of green sticks of wood…

given grudgingly by our large landholders,

who daily held us captive by their conniving ways,

and their unspeakable power and wealth!

Still, we had genuine joy in our hearts

as we'd reap the ripe grains for bread in song,

all with an underling hope,

that our prosperous landlord or Pan

would have no reservations, of eventually sharing some…

to keep our bodies, healthy and strong!

In a way, I felt that fate was definitely on my side

when I was sold to a different Pan to work in that monastery.

That castle of a place on the hilltop, was a real blessing in disguise,

for now I no longer had to labour in the fields

and I felt wildly energized, as though I had won the best prize.

Yes, with that arrangement… I was rather smugly satisfied,

but, the familiar strings of poverty

into which all peasantry folk were doomed,

was not a destiny I wanted to prolong…

either for myself, nor; for my children,

which by the way, I dreamed and hoped…

would very soon, be coming along.

So, to what strange land was I going, you ask?

To tell you the truth, little did I care!

Rumor was, that there were such golden opportunities elsewhere

and I was far from being an immature and imprudent fool

over whose dreamy eyes, one could spin yarns and yarns of fluffy wool.

Reverently, I placed all my trust in God to relocate

and in reality, it really didn't matter where!

(Above) An 1876 lithograph, by artist V.M. Maksumovich. This picture depicts a divide of the family assets. The horse harnesses, furs, kylyms and bolts of cloth are divided amongst the adult children who are leaving home and those remaining. (Below) Pictured, is a more modernistic designed longhaired woolen kylym.

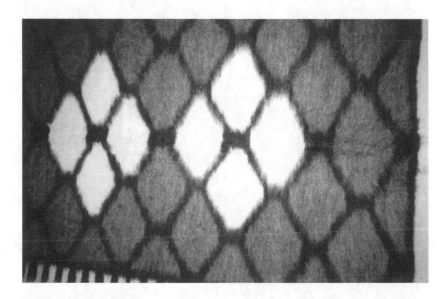

The evening prior to my departure was the great divide…

of cooking utensils, feather pillows and **Ky-lyms***

possessions that my parents could barely spare,

bundled for the voyage and my new life of dreams.

The morning of my send-off came with great trepidation…

for now, I had to say my much-dreaded good-byes.

The expected flood of tears

I determinedly tried to hold back,

but once they gathered, they rolled and they rolled,

their saltiness stung my face and reddened my two eyes!

Suddenly,

I became so acutely aware of a gloomy and ominous revelation,

that… family, friends, as well as my home, I may never be back to see!

This exposé,

I felt compelled to disclose to my nearest and dearest…

for want of reassuring those, whom I knew,

would definitely miss me.

***Ky-lyms** – were homespun wool woven goods such as blankets and rugs.*

Loudly I proclaimed,

"If circumstances be such that we never meet again,

we must not doubt…

The Lord's Greater Plan,

but get out,

get out of Ukraine,

while you still can!"

One final lingering embrace

I gave to each of my two sisters, my brother,

my mother,

and my dear father too,

before departing on that very long journey,

to sail the not so serene ocean blue!

Not knowing what fate had intended

for me,

or any of the others for that matter,

who were leaving that familiar scenic shore,

all with that same profound hope,

of finding something better!

There I was, clutching a few worldly goods,

which happened to also include,

a prized and everlasting remembrance of my homeland;

some **mak ee zem-la,** *or poppy seed and soil,*

tied and concealed in a corner of a hanky tight;

a small but precious gift from my parents,

given with their last tearful parting good-byes.

To closely guard this treasure with all my might,

I tucked it deep into my bosom.

Here it would stay safe from strange prying eyes.

Without looking back, up the gangplank I bravely went…

off to a dismal area called steerage.

There in confinement… where cattle once stood as cargo,

my time aboard would be so forbiddingly spent!

Footnote:

*PAN – was the proper address for those who lead a lordly life, literally translated, it
meant sir, master, or lord. During the tsarist rule, the monarch, along with his nobleman
and the church, owned all the land on which peasantry worked and lived! Thus; all those
who predominated, or reigned over others; were to be properly addressed as Pan, a
derivative from the root of the Ukrainian verb **PA-NU-VA-TY** *that means to predominate,*
to govern, to rule, or lead a lordly life!

Voyage of Fears and Faith

Today, I still can recall that awful nauseating smell…

the smell of manure remnants that here and there

encrusted and clung to the low ceiling and walls,

and the unbearable stench of urine fully penetrating my nostrils,

then leaving me gasping and choking, for more than stale air!

In that barn-like surrounding we were herded there to dwell,

till upon the promised shores of Canada

we waited to land and to musingly stare!

Yes, the sailing ship I boarded was no cruise liner…

though the voyage lasted for a total of fourteen days!

We who stepped onto that pitiful, rickety, groaning vessel…

surrendered our minds to a stupor, or a complete haze!

Conditions were deplorable where we bunked down to nestle

and for lack of suitable rations or meal provisions,

along with the unending swaying and pounding of the rough sea,

all would eventually take its' toll…

in that disgusting place of a hole!

The matter of our rations,

they were without a doubt inadequate.

Identical for all the meals and all the days!

Salty herring and stale dry bread,

making us thirst and cry out for water…Water, WATER,

to relieve the swelling of the head!

By no trosh-ky vo-de*… (Just a little water)…*

a little fresh water, would have stopped or slowed

the tightening of one's throat,

and a head going demented into an uncontrollable craze!

Being such a youngster, it was extremely hard to witness…

the agonizing suffering and then the slow death,

of other village folk I knew…

and with whom on the ship, I so courageously sat!

With such tragic turn of events, a terrifying fear set in,

followed by a cry of resigned desolation, from deep, deep within…

having realized that here, we might just all die!

Yes, my bravery quickly vanished and in my trepidation

for my beloved Ukraine, I did, so repeatedly softly cry!

O-O-O MO-YA U-KRA-YEE-NO! O-O-O MO-YA U-KRA-YEE-NO!

OH MY UKRAINE! OH MY UKRAINE!

Longing the loss of my dear departed friends,

I soon had new company continuously by my side.

Some tiny, wee little things,

which I never had the fortune, or misfortune to see before!

Several people called them **Vo-shy**, *others* **Blo-hy** *(lice, or flees)…*

they too were coming to Canada, and chose us all for their free ride.

Together, we silently anticipated emerging as one,

on the much heard about, Pier 21 of the Great Canadian shore!

I think it was my sheer determination,

or maybe my certainty in God's merciful intervention

happened to be the real reason, that;

He allowed me from the grasps of death to survive…

giving me the strength to bravely step on the shores of Halifax,

when we finally did arrive!

It was extremely difficult to contain my pent-up feelings of grief and fright,

so dreadfully pushed to the pinnacle of a huge explosive climax!

Rapidly new sentiments and mixed emotions in me did quickly vie,

I felt so utterly alone and afraid.

I felt sad, I felt glee,

I felt like a bird released from a cage…

shockingly so carefree,

but oh so grateful and happy,

for being somewhat alive!

The ship's rocking and the rolling had now ceased,

although; my anxiety caused one last retching,

removing the remains of all stomach bile.

Hungry and weak, I staunchly shuffled my lame feet in a dance,

and piercingly a song I did cry… for I was truly pleased.

YA JY-VA, YA JY-VA… YA JY-VA NY-NEE!

I'M ALIVE, I'M ALIVE… I'M ALIVE TODAY!

My victory had me beaming in a smug ear-to-ear smile

and from the bottom of my lungs I loudly shouted…well I'll be!

Unexplainably, the shedding of copious tears followed my outburst and joy!

Following this upsurge of emotions, I was then ready to head for the prairies,

boarding a train for yet another, exhausting five-day journey!

New Adventures in a New Land

Rail destination... Winnipeg!

There I was to meet some emigrants from Ukraine that I knew.

They reassured me they'd help me locate a job

should I ever arrive and find them.

Amazingly, I found those good people,

and on their promise they did follow through.

Unfortunately, unknown to them;

the job where they placed me...

the man was well known,

he was well known

for none other than his inappropriateness and his total meanness!

Without going into detail,

hopefully you know what I'm implying...

but;

relentlessly,

he so demanded,

that I serve him and his house,

in absolute cleanness!

Eight dollars a month was his maximum pay,

twice the amount of the normal going rate,

However,

the food cupboards were

to stay under lock and key the entire whole day!

He also begrudged my asking for a slice of bread for the day,

and me he would so berate.

Maybe,

it was because I was Ukrainian,

that he treated me so badly?

Often,

this I still query!

When I think back,

discrimination against us was rather rampant in the city,

merely because we peasant folk spoke and dressed so differently,

what a pity!

Words,

cannot describe…

the harassment we new immigrants faced at the turn of the century.

Had I not been weighed down

*with so many feelings of **styd**, or shame,*

without a doubt,

from that place I should have packed my things

and immediately run away!

Not knowing the language,

or to whom I should directly complain to by name…

I took all his abuse,

thankful to have a job;

and there in my discontent, I continued to stay.

Nightly I prayed and prayed,

there must be another way!

Low and behold,

*a **vo-rozh-ka** or matchmaker came to say.*

"TUT YE CHO-LO-VEEK,

VEEN BY VAS SHA-NU-VAW!"

(HERE'S A MAN,

HE WOULD LOOK AFTER YOU!)

Glancing at him I plainly knew,

that this 'kid' as a future spouse, just would not do!

He appeared so thin and undernourished,

looking two steps on his way to his own demise,

But, there was something about him rather recognizable,

that made me sigh and then moan,

Hos-po-dy *(Lord God), I loudly cried,*

as I stared into what looked like familiar brown eyes.

I emphatically blurted,

I think I saw you before…

ragged, and daily begging on my street!

Are you not the one from the neighbouring village,

Czarnicie?

Do you have family living in Canada?

I needed immediate clarification,

whether it was he,

who had risked all for me,

in managing to obtain my false passport,

so that in this new world I could be free!

His slow action of nodding his head up and down…

temporarily stopped my heartbeat!

Then he skillfully proceeded to address me…

so proper, so fine,

with such heart-wrenching words…

words, that I think to this day,

I can remember line for line!

What he said to me went something like this…

only if my brain will allow me total recall,

just wait…

it is all coming back now!

Mo-ya Ko-ha-na Ma-ru-sha!

(My Dear Mary!)

By the age of nine, I was orphaned,

and relied on my wit, so death and me would never meet!

From the crack of dawn to nightfall,

I'd make my designated rounds through your village,

hoping to pierce hearts into giving, when,

with these words I would sing, or sometimes call…

DA-YE-TE ME-NEE HLEEB, DA-YE-TE ME-NEE HLEEB,

DA-YE-TE ME-NEE HLEEB, SHCHO-BY BOH VAM-PO-MA-HAW

GIVE ME BREAD, GIVE ME BREAD,

GIVE ME BREAD, SO THAT GOD WILL HELP YOU.

He told me,

we can't escape what fate dishes out,

but we can turn it all on its axis to our aid.

Smiling,

he let me know of something he learned early in life,

and always in his mind to remain ingrained,

that; when, he invoked the mercies of God,

people undeniably were more apt to give,

*an extra slice of bread with **Ka-ly-na*** jam,*

and, thus… another day he would surely live!

But; there were days,

when not a single soul would put any bread into his outstretched hands,

and his spindly legs would collapse beneath him,

when all strength was totally drained!

***Ka-ly-na**-*Wild high bush cranberry that has a very tart and distinct taste.*

Mat-ka Bo-zhy! *(Mother of God) I cried,*

as he had finished telling me of his doomed life!

Then tears of compassion and guilt

commenced to stream uncontrollably down my face,

akin to a threatening cloud bursting into a non-stop pouring rain;

for,

not always did I give him a slice of bread

when he boldly begged to relieve his strife,

my attempts to control the gang of urchins,

that so wanted to 'hang round' our door and windowpane!

In my mind I began to recall,

all my countless self-centered acts…

knowing that I was partly to blame

for his emaciated state, now in full view!

I immediately needed to know,

if he could find it in his heart to forgive me!

But, was fully taken aback by the conversation,

that so long ago, did ensue.

He said he never held it against those who chose not to share,

as he thought of himself as having a lot of street smarts and plenty of finesse,

and that countless opportunities arose daily which he could not always bypass…

the best being the one of becoming a stowaway on a ship sailing to Canada!

Clearly he knew…

if he made this arrangement work, it would definitely spare him

the much-dreaded conscription into an Austrian army regime,

and the mandatory military service for all males, at the young age of sixteen!

He said he saw that occupation as a dead-end job,

figuratively speaking.

Having no desire to emulate an older brother,

who made the army his life,

*begged of him to forge our two passports, ***

in the hope that one-day we'd find each other and marry!

So there he was standing before me,

so proud of himself… telling me we'd make a good team!

If this was a proposal for me to become his life-long mate and mistress,

the thought of him as a possible suitor,

I was wholeheartedly ready to dismiss!

Except,

there was something undeniably captivating and unique

to this charming young fellow!

Wishing to speedily sway the outcome to be more positive,

another tactic on me he'd try.

*From a **tor-ba** or bag,*

he took out a small concertina,

with its bellows turned and awry, saying…

an extremely kind man noticed that when he landed on shore…

having no luggage to claim or tow,

passed him the bag along with this message…

"Go out there, young fellow!

Make music, and then… you'll be a beggar no more!"

Well, on that squeezebox,

he tried so hard to play a melodious tune or two…

*haunting songs, of **Sta-ree Krye** or the old country.*

A wave of lonesomeness overcame me,

making my heartache and me ever so blue!

The memories he evoked of my homeland skies

I wished at that moment not to be inclined.

Thus it was best, that this utterly strange encounter...

or bizarre meeting; be shelved, in the far back of my mind.

As far as romancing with this fellow, I was far from being keen.

According to my passport, where my birth was falsely signed

I was soon to be eighteen, but in all reality, hardly sixteen!

He, I might reckon, a couple of years my junior,

maybe a mere thirteen or fourteen...

though real good looking,

with such entrancing, warm, twinkling dark brown eyes.

Indeed, he was strikingly handsome,

with a heart so enormous and so majestically kind!

I'm sure that if any woman was seeking a man,

this one for certain, she'd fall head over heals and idolize.

As for me, I was completely baffled as to why...

why destiny had put him on my path?

He was in such need of a mother...and I,

in need of pleasing my growing despondent spirit!

To remedy my situation,

another cleaning job I would start like no other.

I soon began to enjoy my life,

caring for a butcher man's house

as well as his high-class, charming dear wife!

They were friendly, lavishly offering more, than plenty to eat,

and the variety of food the butcher nightly brought home…

was beyond a doubt, for me, a Real Grand Treat!

Sliced ham, baloney, salami, and garlic sausages galore…

but feeling so lost, so forlorn, and so incomplete,

my downcast heart continued to secretly long, for something more!

Then my physical health plummeted, as I could no longer eat!

The effects of my melancholic syndrome left me totally drained,

leaving me too weak to carry out a day's work

for which I was somewhat significantly paid and trained.

My new employer noticed, that…

over the next few months my big appetite daily waned.

My cheeks became ever more hollow,

my face so drawn, so etched, so pained!

The butcher desperately wanted to know…

just what could be so gravely wrong?

Hoping he could be of some help,

I wept thru tears,

lamenting in song.

Send me back to my country,

send me back to my home,

send me back to my family,

for here I am, so all alone!

Oh how I miss my dear mother,

who cried a million tears.

How I miss my dear father,

who reassured all my fears

and I miss my little brother,

my sisters and all my kin,

and each day that I am here,

something dies so deep within.

Footnote:

This young child, orphaned at the age of ten went to live with his eldest brother Dominco, who at the age of forty had taken his first wife. Dominco's wife, who married for the first time in her later years as well, had great difficulties in adjusting to a child living with her and her newly married spouse! This arrangement was a responsibility Dominco's wife did not relish, as she absolutely loathed children! Thus, she made her dislike known to this child in many mean ways, on somewhat of a daily basis. Dominco, often away from home on military assignments; had no knowledge of the ill treatment his wife lashed out on his little brother. Receiving continual rejection from such an uncaring woman, this young boy ran away from his brother's home and took to the streets to fend for himself! The generosity of strangers not only kept him alive but also fulfilled the need to feel loved by someone, even though it were total strangers; and through their kindness, he managed to stay alive and not become a street mortality. His dream was always to reconnect to his other unknown siblings, brothers: Peter, or John, or sisters, Magdaline and Marynka, all of whom had emigrated from Ukraine when he was just an infant. His sister Marynka left to Parana, Brazil where she met and married a Mikola Pressner. His other siblings all married in Ukraine and with their spouses tried to make a life. With poverty looming, all left with their growing families simultaneously to Canada, in search of the free land.

Leery of the kind of person his sister's spouse in Brazil might be, and not wanting to ever again, be caught up in a predicament that drove him out into the streets, he felt his best bet would be to connect to his family in Canada. He knew that his sister Magdaline and her husband, John Hocaluk, along with his two brothers, Peter and John, had with their spouses and children taken up the free homesteads in the Municipality of Brokenhead, all to live within close proximity to each other.

If only he could find these Canadian siblings, they would surely welcome him, as he would
offer his labour free, and so spare them some of the hard work in establishing their farms.

Hearing, that his idolized friend, Mary; was seriously thinking of emigrating, his plans
became more well thought-out, seeking the help of his military brother to carry out the
arrangement of their customized passports! Neither of their truthful ages would have
allowed them to become a candidate for legal immigration without the presence of an adult
family member. To speed up the process of their going to Canada, it was vital that they both
had an altered passport, for he so wanted to be entitled to a free homestead. With the two black-
market passports in hand, judiciously he set his mind on what next he must do, should the most
opportune time present itself to emigrate!

My Grandfather's pearl button Horner accordion has gracefully aged, the bellows
hold air but there are some wood components that are held together with string.

A Life Changing Incident

Well,

I didn't mean to put the butcher man in such an awkward position,

He sat there a long time,

shaking his head and contemplating as to what next he should do.

Finally, his plan was that the matchmaker should quickly return.

She unquestioningly did,

escorting none other… than the same guy,

who had previously tried, so gallantly me to woo!

Yes, that unbelievable young guy,

except this time he was all spiffed up and so handsome was he!

Dressed in a hat and sporting a tie,

he was a far cry from that shabby émigré!

Amazingly,

he had no resemblance to that previous beanpole of a scrawny kid.

Right there in front of my eyes

stood a well-formed man…and heaven forbid,

I had a slight change of heart,

something that only, we women can!

Except, to my knowledge, he was still a fulltime begging orphan…

and what in God's Name, could this vagabond really offer me?

Bearing gifts of chocolates,

he asked me for my hand, telling me…

"I just paid ten dollars,

TEN DOLLARS;

FOR A HUNDRED AND SIXTY, ACRES OF LAND!"*

"DE-SHYAT DO-LA-RYW;

(TEN DOLLARS;)

SHCHO-BY MO-YA ZHEEN-KA MA-LA FAR-MU!"

(SO THAT MY WIFE WILL HAVE FARM!)

To this second more serious proposal,

yet so out of the blue;

I justly wrestled with my heart.

Being homesick and depressed,

I wasn't sure what I wanted,

or exactly, what I should do!

*The one hundred and sixty acre homesteads were free, but a ten-dollar fee

was required of each homesteader to process the governmental paper work!

But surely,

it would have been rather foolish of me

to turn down a young man with a farm…

so, a more favourable answer I did give him,

as we tenderly embraced,

and bid our adieu.

In less than a week's time,

we both shopped and we packed

and now were ready to depart,

despite the many grave warnings from our friends, who…

all felt, we were in need of a good talking to!

To our city acquaintances,

the thought of going off into the wilderness was less than brainy.

They told us, that; our plan was a poor cure

to lighten our lonesomeness and just plain zany,

in fact, somewhat **Ku-ku-ree-ku,**

literally,

it would incite the laughter of a rooster!

Their counsel went totally unheeded!

With a hundred pounds of supplies loaded on our backs,

we were off to trudge the shores of the river north,

over fixed and timeworn Native tracks!

Our anticipation urged us forward, inch-by-inch,

on that treacherous fifty-mile hike,

and by some unknown means we walked, non-stop…

for roughly thirty hours,

en route to locate and lay claim to…

the buried surveyor's land spike!

Yes, with our hopes and dreams we finally arrived,

knowing little about a chicken, or a cow,

but at last here we were…

to be transformed into pioneer farmers and eke out a living,

somehow!

Silently, we were both thinking, could we endure this wilderness?

So inhospitable appeared this foreign place!

This free land of bush, rock, swamp and mosquitoes!

Lots of mosquitoes, whose gnawing bites drove us to near madness!

Shielding our hands and face, we begged the Almighty for His mercy and grace.

Suddenly, our joint thoughts dwelt on how we had been mislead

and tears abruptly spilt over to wash my swollen bitten face.

Maybe the idea of being farmers, we could perhaps rescind?

Soon a glimmer of hope came from the summer winds that sang from afar,

as they bent and bowed the tall treetops, rustling the leaves,

to create a continual hushed whisper of grace.

The canopy of dense foliage, that so totally obliterated the sun's rays;

seemed to be whispering a blessing with each gust of wind.

A sort of benediction, sent forth to the benevolent Great Creator…

to approve and guide us! Guide us green and inexperienced

Hos-po-de-nya ee Hos-po-dar, *(Stewards of the land)*

and help make this, our permanent family homestead.

Full of faith and self-determination, along with willing backs and spines,

we hurriedly started the task of building our abode... a small log house.

Sod for a roof and sod for a floor, our humble home stood without delay,

welcoming all...with one cock-eyed and crooked, petite window and door!

This was not a mansion, but it kept the hungry eyes of the howling wolves at bay!

Previously, they fearlessly crept closer and closer to our carefully placed branches of pines

under which we collapsed at days end from exhaustion, near the damp earth floor.

At least now, we could sleep in peace

without the petrifying thoughts of wolves swallowing us whole.

There was a chance that from the elements and wildlife we'd survive,

but how exactly were we to live when we had nothing?

O-ye Bo-zhy! *(Oh God!)*

A joint passionate dream that seemed to rapidly transpire,

we had no choice but to put aside.

That off…

officially becoming sanctified as husband and wife!

Currently our prime concern was…

how in God's name were we to stay alive?

Hopelessness began to give way to despair,

but, by surrendering ourselves,

the world conspired to provide all.

Neighbours hurriedly came to our aid, in grand fair!

Generously, they offered what little they had…

as survival was dependent

on the sowing and the sharing of…

Our Daily Bread!

In this expatriate community,

most of our daily troubles became rather small.

Feeling safe and accepted,

our fears miraculously receded,

as incredible goodwill spread.

Old European feuds and historical hatreds

were immediately put aside,

making entrenched bitter hearts grow and swell…

with an unprecedented and unknown, fashionable pride!

No matter what language,

religion,

or nationality one happened to be…

It was through the sharing of bread that we became one,

much like a huge family!

Settling amongst the Natives,

bez hro-shee

(without money),

they showed us exactly what to gather,

from the wild… and eat for free.

Quickly all nationalities blended…English, French,

Irish, Icelandic, Norwegian,

Ukrainian, Polish,

Czechoslovakian, German, and Jew.

Together we formed a building bee

to build places of worship, communities, and schools,

for the benefit of everyone, not just for a few,

as Freedom and Democracy were now The New Rules!

At the end of the day,

neighbours would gather to sing, to dance, and even to pray,

all these spontaneous happenings, as if on cue!

This tremendous goodwill

of caring and sharing amongst most of the neighbours,

often brought stern warnings and consternation

from each respective church!

"One will not marry

or celebrate services in another's house of faith,

as doing so would place one's soul

in a precarious position, or perch!"

Ohe vhye (*Oh boy*), *our ears to those messages …we did not incline,*

nor did we fear the power of those pulpit sermons, delivered so fine.

Instead, we continued to place our trust in God and in neighbour,

for one could not betray the extraordinary bond of communion that arose,

from our frequent sharing of work, bread, and homemade mead wine.

This so expanded our hearts into a bond with our neighbours,

in an abiding unity of loyalty, faithfulness and brotherly love…

that in a short period of time,

new families of race, of culture, and of religion evolved,

surely blessed by Him, who had united us together, from above!

In Canada, many of our old ways…

especially the taboos and fears of being ostracized

by the church, by neighbours, or some other social order and class,

all seemed to play less of a role. Our spirits were grasped by a new awakening,

that being, our need for each other, and from this, a sharing community evolved!

We had come to a new landmass, and literally, we were all still on the same boat,

as sheer survival was our primary goal!

All those time-aged taboos and fears, with which we had been raised;

were no longer allowed to worry, or to occupy, our busy waking days!

In Canada Blessings Abound

Ko-ma-ree vje ne ma, *(The mosquitoes are gone,)*

ee zym-nee vee-ter du-ye veed peew-neech na zymu

(and the cold north winds announce the coming of winter),

blowing right through all the unstopped gaps of our little house at night.

But;

our many blessings we daily counted and tallied,

with such sheer delight!

The land we had chosen grew huge rocks,

scattered and seeded everywhere like wild

and was literally covered with thousands of trees

of every description and size, for firewood to be filed and then piled!

Lacking access to the forest for fuel was the norm in Ukraine,

thus with both building and heating commodities right next to our door,

as well as having such remarkable good neighbours,

there wasn't much else to be asking, or beseeching God for…

other than maybe, which trees not to unearth

so as to keep those stones buried forever, under the rich black dirt!

Endeavouring to work and function in harmony

many blessings transpired upon each and every one of us!

We were all struggling to make a new life in a new country,

and disunity would only have brought more unbearable strife upon us!

On this new soil, we had the opportunity to also start afresh, or anew,

in the building of a more humane and peaceful future,

for generations yet to come!

Thus, through random acts of kindness,

along with the sharing of one's skills and resources,

a new life of camaraderie and community commenced to daily ensue.

Because of this genuine generosity,

all but the weakest survived the ordeal of being a pioneer

in that daunting wilderness!

It amazingly seemed like a dream…

that we had such good neighbours

who, at the most appropriate time;

always appeared, to just drop by…

for barn raising, quilting, and aiding in the cutting,

of our small patch, of harvest-ready rye!

But more astonishing was having land so grand,

something unimaginable

DLYA DVA KRY-PA-KEEW

(for two serfs or peasant labourers),

bound to and transferred with the sale of all farm land,

a practice carried out by those wealthy feudal landowners

in our far-off, native, Ukrainian homeland!

Before an icon,

gracefully draped with my own hand embroidered towel or **rush-nyk***…*1st*

an icon of the Mother of God with the Divine Child Jesus,

personifying the kindness of God,

there we stood,

singing songs of thanksgiving in celebration of our milestone!

At the top of our lungs we sang praises for the gift of God's faithful promises,

for the gift of our neighbours continual heartfelt loving ways

and for the gift of bountiful land that one day we could call our very own,

at which time our burdening troubles would be transformed

into one of the happiest and sweetest, smelling bouquets!

Unknowingly, our melancholy for our beloved Ukraine began to subside…

With each passing day,

there were fewer tears to wipe on the back of one's shirtsleeve

or from one's friends shamefully hide,

as we took up ownership of what was at hand…

becoming Canadians in this foreign land!

Yes, our deep longing for our dear and beloved Ukraine incredibly did abate

as we experienced this rare living testament

of what people could achieve, *2nd

when survival so hinged on neighbours,

needing to come together and to daily co-operate!

That is not to say that those weren't challenging pioneer days,

living in the middle of nowhere,

waking with the fear of having nothing to eat…

along with the many other trials

that undeniably tested our strength in our faith.

In due course, it slowly did happen…

No-vy-ye reed-nee-yee deem*!*

(A new native homeland!)

Thus,

when our relatives from back home

would write the occasional letter,

insistently pleading, that…

we'd return back to the old country,

and bring an end to all their worries,

fearful that we would perish in the sub-zero cold,

or worse,

succumb to a slow and miserable starvation.

It was then, that…

we shared less of our troubles to halt their dreadful thoughts,

extolling the virtues of our new homeland as being,

way beyond our own doubting expectation.

There were a few

who couldn't adapt or cut the mustard,

returning from where they came.

The ruggedness of that life was more than they could bear

and mighty quick had left the scene…

never to be seen on their homestead again!

But we stuck it out,

with the hope of a brighter future,

for generations to come,

Knowing that…this newfound freedom

would be worth the price of all our pain!

Gradually,

to our new native homeland Canada,

accolades we would sing or hum.

TSE-YE NA-SHE U-KRA-YEE-NA!

TSE-YE NA-SHE U-KRA-YEE-NA!

TSE-YE NA-SHE NO-VEE KRA-YE!

(THIS IS OUR UKRAINE!

THIS IS OUR UKRAINE!

THIS IS OUR NEW COUNTRY!)

SLA-VA BOH-HO!

(PRAISE GOD!)

Footnotes:

- *1*[st]

Rush-nyk *or rush-nyky (more than one) are embroidered towels of varying lengths. These towels are richly embroidered and are typically made with either intricate geometric designs or floral motifs stitched with bright red thread onto near white homespun linen.*

The embroidered towels played a very significant role in the day-to-day life of a Ukrainian home, somewhat akin to prayer shawls. A more affluent family would have many towels, one for each living member of that household! When these towels were not in use in various ceremonial rituals, they loosely framed religious icons that graced the walls of one's home!

A towel would usually follow each child from birth to death, becoming the first swaddling clothing that wrapped a newborn, later placed to hang over an icon, close to where the infant slept. Should the child become gravely ill, the towel was once again placed around the child during a prayer vigil carried out by the family. When illness or death descended upon one's house, a longer towel was wound around gatepost to gatepost. This ritual was carried out as a final measure to ward-off the evil spirits. The belief was, that these evil spirits bringing illness could strike the entire family, if so allowed to go unchecked at the gate. Thus, this towel needed to have sufficient length to seal off the property! Upon the death of a family member, the embroidered towel adorned the hand-hewn casket. In the cemetery it served as the device to lower the deceased below grade and in the end, it too, was placed in its final resting place, draped over the wooden cross marker to blow in the wind. Towels were also used in happier times. Customarily, a young bride wore her towel as a head cover during the marriage vows, later the towel bound her hands to those of her spouse, now entering the world as one!

During any calendar year, the towel most definitely would have adorned the family table at both Christmas and Easter, taking its place of honour as the uppermost tablecloth at the family meal.

- *2ⁿᵈ*

The former Governor General, Right Honourable Ed. Schreyer who grew up in this community once commented in a public address, "the League of Nations along with the rest of society would operate more smoothly, had they experienced the cohesiveness of this multi-cultural community, with neighbour helping neighbour! A development that started with the early pioneers and still continues to this very day."

This elaborately embroidered Rush-nyk was purchased in an open street market of Ukraine.

·❖· *Part Two* ·❖·

The Strings of Life Play On

Ves-na pry-ho-dy

(Spring is coming)

and on a day when it wasn't too cold,

across the swamp we went,

stepping cautiously on the newly laid cordwood roads

so that we'd arrive at the church without incident

and exchange our wedding bands of gold!

Crowned in my **Vee-nok**, or bridal headpiece

made of braided flowers, herbs, and garlic, tied with flowing ribbons,

and; wearing my most exquisite artistically woven skirt or **Plakh-ta**,

which was by then splattered with mud to mid-thigh,

we alone marched down the church aisle.

My heart so ached for my family… I just knew; I was going to cry.

My closest kin were absent, to approve of my choice with their smile

and intone the customary Blessing or **Bla-ho-slo-ve-nya!**

Soon, stinging tears of my disappointment would not abate…

but the priest carried on saying, "Mary Wyhrysta; do you take this man…

Michael Smolinski, as your life-long husband and mate?"

In haste I blurted,

Beeh-me! *(For sure!)*

I should have really said "I Do!"

Anyway, with those two little words…we were wed!

This sanctioned union,

finally put an end to all our neighbours' speculations…

whether the two of us would one day share a straw mattress,

as our soft, bridal bed!

Our good-willed neighbours, we invited them all,

to attend an unforgettable celebration,

this took place at the house that we managed to build the previous fall.

Tut my hosh-tee pry-ye-ma-ly stym har-nu ze-le-nu yush-ku.

(Here our guests we welcomed with a special green juice.)

The recipe to make that exceptional drink was simple,

even to the totally unskilled.

In the sun, several wooden buckets were set to percolate,

with the residual slime from tobacco leaves, just freshly squeezed,

and to their brim, those pails were ever so filled!

In approximately ten days time,

this green liquid was ready to mix with something

the **go-ver-man** *sold and distilled.*

This made a powerful concoction or drink,

a quick panacea for all life's worries and every wrong,

for it so impeded one's ability to rationally think,

priming one to let loose of their qualms in dance and in song!

For the whole weekend the festivity was sustained

by dancing many a **Ko-lo-my-ye-ka***… **

a brisk dance made lively and swift

on an assortment of homemade white spruce violins!

With their taut waxed bows of horsetail hair

the musicians played and played…

and our little house became like a hostel or a hotel,

in a mighty quick makeshift,

accommodating all who forgot the way home

and just stayed, and stayed!

*****Ko-lo-my-ye-ka** *-Upbeat spirited circle dance that is typically danced at many*

a traditional Ukrainian wedding!

*A **Da-ru-nok** or gift*

was presented to us by each of our friends upon entering our doorway.

Some people gave us freshly baked small loaves of bread * 1st.

*or **Bu-bloch-ky**. * 2nd.*

so we'd not hunger during periods of terrible strife.

*Others gave us **Py-san-ky**, *3rd. or decorated eggs,*

both of these, to us Ukrainians,

are somewhat highly revered, as symbols "of our life."

Then there were those who presented us with either money

*or homemade potato **sa-ma-hon-ka**…a type of self-warming water,*

better known as alcohol spirits or vodka today.

The medicinal use of this clear firewater

was much tooted to bring on a renewed vitality

and move one's spirits to see a clearer headway.

Contrary to beliefs, nothing did it energize or quell!

Instead, it seized its allowing victims to dance with demons,

who in turn, flung them into an abyss…

of their very own, man-made; private hell!

We were ingenious in our search for instant happiness.

All done to free one from their burdening worries, sorrows, or pain!

Except; ultimately, the frequent use of alcohol spirits

caused the downfall of many an individual, along with their family,

as the addiction grasped one's mind and took over,

and thereby, superbly in a tight stronghold, it would daily reign.

But, whether there were gifts or no gifts,

and as to their suitability, it really mattered little …

for we had learned from our despairing isolation,

life's surest and most important uplifts…

were the opportunities for neighbour to gather with neighbour

and that, for a few fleeting moments… life to celebrate!

It was amazing, how time and time again,

the sharing of mutual difficulties and troubles…

would cause those looming crises to magically abate!

Frequently, one's own rocky plight was soon forgotten, especially when…

embraced by the support of neighbours and their camaraderie,

and laughter would prevail, relinquishing one, yet once again,

from an emotional pain, caused by the broken ties, of home and family.

Our celebration was just that kind of event,

neighour, meeting with neighbour, to talk things over!

Then, there were those

who repetitively presented,

in song and in verse,

many heartfelt good wishes,

to us… the bride and groom!

Da-ye Bo-zhy! *(To God!)*

Na Shcha-Stya! *(For Good Luck!)*

Na Zda-row- ya! *(For Good Health!)*

And many children of course…to come along soon,

all with an earnest hope of creating,

one hell' of a prosperous BOOM!

Yes,

to both of us they toasted and sang lots of **DA-YE BO-ZHY**…

asking God to grant a long life,

in perpetual good health

but more importantly, numerous children…

who would eventually generate, a new flourishing wealth!

Most mothers agreed and told me, that;

each child would bring new joys to my heart,

moreover, the more I had,

the more helpful they would be!

Especially when they grow older… "They'll be your hope!"

others confirmed… "They'd be immeasurable,

in giving the family farm a fantastic start; you'll see!"

But, I was most mindful of the moms with ten or more children,

Bo-zhy mee *(My God), how exactly did they cope?*

Our wedding was spectacular!

Had a socialite reporter been invited,

the morning newspaper headlines would have read…

UKRAINIANS KNOW HOW TO PARTY

AND WEDDINGS ARE EXCEPTIONALLY HEARTY!

A three-day event with music, song,

Ko-ba-sa ee Ko-ro-vaye **4ᵗʰ.for all;*

(Sausage and Wedding bread)

But drinks for those who knew how to drink,

or were somewhat resiliently hardy!

Tak; ee py-ty nad tee sho sna-ly-yak!

(Indeed; drinks for only those who knew how to drink!)

For all knew too well,

just what that green mixed-up whiskey would do…

filling one's eyes with a tear or two,

as such was its powerful kick,

followed by a deep sleep of several hours, or days, and then…

making one, so dreadfully and unpleasantly sick!

The party took on a life of its own,

by those who could play or sing… The Old Songs,

that were memorized and passed down from one generation to the next,

worthy instructions or knowledge,

on how not to get overly vexed!

Typical instructional songs,

sung at a Ukrainian wedding in your Baba's day

usually contained a message

for a new bride to note and to heed,

"How to conquer your man…

to provide the loving all women need."

An old favorite of mine I'll sing for you now,

in English if I may.

My auntie's, they did tell me,
a long, long, time ago…
you want your man to love you,
there's something you must do.
CHORUS   Make him lots of py-ro-hy, py-ro-hy, py-ro-hy!
*   Make him lots of py-ro-hy*
*   and then he will love you!*

They also happened to mention,
if you wanted him to perform;
you mustn't let him go hungry,
or he'll become forlorn.
CHORUS   Make him lots of py-ro-hy, py-ro-hy, py-ro-hy!
*   Make him lots of py-ro-hy*
*   and then he will love you!*

So if you want your marriage,
to be a life of bliss
go home and plant potatoes,
and then follow this!
CHORUS   Make him lots of py-ro-hy, py-ro-hy, py-ro-hy!
*   Make him lots of py-ro-hy*
*   and then he will love you!*

To make sure you got the message
the message of this song
two more times I'll sing the refrain
and you must sing along.
CHORUS   Make him lots of py-ro-hy, py-ro-hy, py-ro-hy!
*   Make him lots of py-ro-hy*
*   and then he will love you!*

There you have it!

The recipe to keep one's marriage on a continuous up swing,

handed down from many generations past.

It's those irresistible **Py-ro-hy***, * 5th.*

that make a marriage last!

Sadly, our festive wedding finally concluded.

Albeit, the most satisfying part of that night was…

knowing that we waited!

Until we mutually made plans to wed,

I had no amorous desires for this man.

Initially, I impulsively agreed

to join him as his wedded wife on his homestead,

but, my unending lonesomeness for my family and village

required nothing more of him, other than his companionship.

I thought you may want to know that, but back to the wedding pre-finale.

As soon as the last of the partying guests departed,

we headed out on a type of patrol for one-second look…

to check that no one was left sleeping in the bush, you know,

or by off chance fell near the cold running brook!

A couple of children had seen two people

behind the woodpile, barely dressed,

then running deep into the forest

over the remaining drifts of snow!

Someone told them…

*"The **CH-ORT** or devil must be chasing them,"*

and to be safe…past the garden gate they must not go.

Hearing this, I cracked up in a spasm of convulsive laughter.

Ha, ha, ha…ha, ha, ha… ha, ha, ha.

Ya sure, a 'ch-ort' chasing them!

My laughter caused the voice of my Baba to recede,

and I could clearly hear my Uncle, now speaking once again!

Listening to the next part of his conversation,

my Uncle was quick to reveal, that the wedding celebration

remained a cherished memory for his parents,

as they stepped back into their harsh existence

in trying to deal with the grave realities of life.

But, the much bigger issue… was that of the money shortage!

Footnotes:

1st. To Ukrainians, bread is not only a daily staple, but is also one of the holiest of all the food groups. In a Ukrainian home, great reverence is shown to this staple, never to be discarded in the garbage or thrown about carelessly. Because of this reverence, bread dough to be shaped for baking was invariably made into many creative forms and usually elaborately decorated in some fashion. In the baking of the bread a cook pressed for time would simply apply an egg wash prior to its removal from the oven and this would liven-up the dull crust into one with a highly polished sheen! Poppy seeds sprinkled on crust tops were often standard fare, but if time was not of essence, the bread dough was shaped and braided into elaborate huge circles, this was to denote the circle of one's eternity. These fancier braided ring-shaped bread loaves, better known as **Ka-lach or **Ko-lach**, would traditionally grace the table on all family celebrations and religious holidays. Today, because many households have under-gone major lifestyle changes; this egg rich circle of bread is less frequently seen, other than, on **Shva-ty Ve-chyr** or Holy Night. On the eve of Christmas three-braided bread loaves are stacked, one upon another in adoration to the Trinity, and in the middle of these loaves, a candle is lit to signifying the light Jesus brought into the world.*

*A much lighter bread dough version, containing many a raisin is baked for the holiday celebrations of Easter and is better known as the **Pas-ka**. If the bread dough is made superbly fine in texture as in a cake batter it is better known as a **Ba-ba** or **Bab-ka**. These breads are also made with many eggs to produce a golden yellow colour, and; to increase the colour intensity and flavour, saffron is added, if it is readily available! On Easter Sunday morning, this bread is the center most element of the family table and has a central motif of one dough cross, symbolic of Christ's crucifixion and our salvation. Baked in tall cylindrical containers it towers above the blessed boiled eggs, colorful **Py-sanky** (decorated eggs) and sausage that make this simple sunrise meal superb!*

The most elaborate of breads are those baked for a wedding celebration! Traditionally, these are two circular loaves of bread, adorned with ornate tiny doves! The shape of the bread loaves, along with the painstakingly placed doves denote an unending love that each spouse will have for the other spouse, till their parting death. These loaves are brought to the church and used as part of the marriage rite. At the wedding celebration, the loaves are cut and shared as one, with the celebrating guests.

To persons of Ukrainian heritage and culture, bread is definitely the staff of life, to be shared as a measure of welcome when one receives guests into one's home. To drop-in as a guest, especially into one's newly established home, it is traditionally correct to bring along a loaf of bread, to be placed into their kitchen cupboard with an everlasting wish for the inhabitants. The wish expressed to the occupying household members is simply, that never would they be in want of this staple.

*2ⁿᵈ.

Bu-bloch-ky – *Small round buns, so feather light in texture that one could eat a dozen by oneself. If these feather light buns had a filling of either prunes, sauerkraut, or a mixture of cottage cheese and potatoes they then acquired the name of* **Py-ryzh-ky**

*3ʳᵈ.

Py-san-ky- *Artistically designed eggs with many symbols. Each line and symbol is made with a heated fine nib-writing tool called a kistka that is filled with bee's wax to write the cryptic messages. For the receiver of this prize egg, these messages denote some wish for their life, such wishes were a combination of health, wealth, and longevity. After each series of writings the egg is placed into alternating brilliant dye colours, the final colour usually being, jet-black!*

With the last colour wash on, the final step that completes the writing of the egg is the step whereby, the wax lines are all stripped off the egg. The wax stripping is accomplished by holding the egg close to a candle flame, the soon melting wax is wiped off. Magically, the completed egg reveals its beauty to the writer. The methodical and painstaking efforts of one's creative writing are never disappointments. It is believed that this glorious transformation in the egg is somewhat symbolic of the transformation that awaits all who live and die in Christ. It is for this reason that these written eggs are greatly revered as a symbol of life!

*4th.

Ko-ro-vaye - *A fancy wedding bread used as part of the ritual when a couple take their marriage vows.*

*5th.

Py-ro-hy *-or perogies, is a name that Canadians commonly use to describe soft-boiled dough dumplings, but their rightful name is* **Ve-re-ny-ky**, *true* **Py-ro-hy** *are baked not boiled. These doughy dumplings are made with a multiple of fillings. The most common fillings used are potato, or potatoes and cheese. When boiled they are served smothered with butter, onions, and sour cream!*

EASY RECIPE FOR SIX-DOZEN OF DELECTABLE PEROGIES

750 ml flour (3 cups)	*250ml warm water (1cup)*
80ml vegetable oil (1/3cup)	*5ml salt (1teaspoon)*

METHOD: *Combine the above and kneed well, cover for a ½ hour rest. Then, divide dough into six even balls. Work with one ball, roll to the thickness of 1/8 inch. Cut with a cookie cutter. In center of circle dough, place 1 tsp. of filling. (below) Then seal edges.*

FILLING: *Mash 2 1/2 cups hot potatoes with 3/4cup grated cheddar cheese.*

COOKING: *Place 2 dozen in 4 liters of boiling salted water (1tsp) boil slowly, for2-4min. Do not cover! Stir Gently. Remove when floating, drain Add pre-fried buttered onions.*

These ornately decorated breads and Py-san-ky were an exhibit seen at the Kiev Pavilion during Folklarama, a multicultural festival that has been held in the city of Winnipeg for the past twenty-five years. These cultural displays were made available for the festival celebrations on behalf of, the Ukrainian Cultural and Education Center, Winnipeg, Manitoba

Home Alone

Clearing his throat, my Uncle continued, "Homesteading was tough;

I don't know if you're aware, that, in the early years;

many farmers from Manitoba left home in search of seasonal work,

sometimes walking or hopping a boxcar of a train; to the northern states,

Ontario, or Saskatchewan, in order to find a paying job.

They looked for any type of employment to make that extra dollar or two!

They were in desperate need of cash to make purchases of small implements.

But, more crucial was the need to buy the basic necessities…

staples like flour and sugar, so as to be able to survive in that wilderness.

With no paying work nearby,

your Grandpa left home in search of employment too,

shortly after the wedding celebrations!

Boy oh boy, such confidence he placed in his new young bride,

leaving a woman all alone at home…

as he roamed miles and miles, looking for manual labour!

He went straight south,

and landed a job as a farmhand for several months…

I think in the state of North Dakota.

But, while your Baba stayed behind,

she apparently led a life of great disorder!

She occasionally spoke of her so-called hunting days.

How she'd scavenge the forest from sunrise to sundown,

for anything she could find to eat!

Except,

those few wild mushrooms and berries were a poor substitute

*for a bowl full of **Ka-sha** or buckwheat, with a little bit of meat!*

You know…

she just about died from hunger."

When my Uncle began to tell me…

of how afraid and lonesome his mother must have felt…

living by herself in the bush, and that maybe, just maybe,

she lacked the necessary survival skills to make it on her own.

It was then, that; I could hear my Baba's voice!

First, softly entering in,

but dramatically increasing in volume,

as she told the next part of her story,

of her being, home alone!

Tak sa-mot-na ya sta-la…

(Indeed so lonesome I got…)

being extremely isolated in my far-off little house

but, frequently visited by… A STRANGE MAN!

A real eccentric, bitter louse,

who would scare me something terrible.

Jolting me, from all my intellectual wits!

For some unknown reason

he had found it completely amusing…

to hang dead skunks on my door,

till finally the day came when I knew,

I could not take this, for a minute more.

I would definitely have to swallow my pride and call it quits!

Heavens, winter was fast approaching and,

the unwelcome cold was creeping right through the closed door.

Worse yet, there wasn't any food to eat!

De cho-lo-veek?

(Where was my man?)

He had been gone far too long

and only he knew how to hunt for meat!

Repeatedly, I pleaded to God about my doomed plight,

O-ye Bo-zhy, O-ye Bo-zhy,

(Oh God, Oh God,)

seeking comfort,

to relieve some of my fast impinging and immobilizing fright!

I was afraid, I was hungry, and I was lonesome!

I had an unrelenting fear

that my spouse was unhappy with our marriage and decided not to return,

or maybe, he had found another woman.

Even worse,

I feared him to be dead!

Other migrant workers had returned weeks earlier,

and had no word of his whereabouts!

It was as if he had disappeared from the face of the earth.

I guess you might say I had my share of hardships,

some real and some imagined.

But, the last straw was…

that my long summer labours of drying mushrooms and berries were,

NOWHERE TO BE FOUND!

My winter provisions had mysteriously vanished…

leaving the larder completely empty,

consumed by rats and mice, which shared my tiny space, a plenty!

A quick decision I had to make,

as starvation would become imminent,

if leave from that place I did not to take…

before my energy was totally spent.

Tak *(Indeed),*

frozen ground would yield little or nothing over the long winter haul.

Firstly,

I had a score to settle with those mice,

for they had robbed me blind!

Amongst them I strategically seated myself…

to reprimand all for their brave wayward ways,

only to be confronted by the most unimaginable instead,

which by the way,

for many a day;

had so completely

BOGGLED MY MIND!

Mice giggling, singing, and dancing

as if mocking me for their smart and dodgy plays…

then changing into faceless people

reluctant to share a morsel of bread when I repeatedly begged!

One slice, one slice of crusty dry bread…I overwhelmingly cried,

attempting to put an end to my mind's dreadful haze!

Yes,

I was literally starving

but much too embarrassed by this whole mouse fiasco

to say even one word to any of my neighbours!

I know,

that had they known of my dire predicament

they surely would have helped me.

But,

how could I tell them?

I had nothing to eat!

Or,

the unbelievable,

how mice had ridiculed me after eating all my winter staples!

For many a day,

I often wondered about that whole episode,

although today,

I know better.

It was all a hallucination or madness

that took over my body,

as I was so dreadfully undernourished!

Transforming Events

At once, in a small satchel,

I placed a few things that I had…

the empty frying pan and soup pot from the kitchen,

along with the pillows and the coverings from the bed.

I was then ready to head out from my protective front door!

But,

in my scurry to pack,

an extreme tiredness overcame me.

Plainly, this inertia became incredibly difficult, to just ignore.

On the spur of the moment,

I laid my head so very sad,

for one last time,

upon my stripped marital bed!

My ominous thoughts gave way to a weary sleep,

with many a disturbing dream,

then a series of thundering knocks,

first once, then twice, and again and again,

making me suddenly bolt from my bed with a loud cry and a scream!

*"**Toy naz-da-lee lu-dy-na!**"*

("That good for nothing person") I loudly shrieked, thinking…

it could be no one else but the skunk man,

attaching yet another dead skunk to my door!

Anger drove me into a wild rage and I knew not what… I should do.

But, swiftly I snapped into action… for we were at war!

In that very split second, I audaciously knew,

I must have the final revenge

on that uncivilized, Skunk Man Creep!

A lesson, he'll long remember and see-through.

Determined to carry out a plan of attack,

I quickly ran with a kitchen knife to the door…

I opened the latch ever so cautiously,

just enough for me to have a real fast peep!

There before me, a man had stood,

with a gun on one shoulder and an axe on the other!

Terrified as to what exactly he might do next,

I needed to strike first,

so he'd surprise me no more!

Turning cold with fear,

my heart pounded and rapidly did race…

probably in those same circumstances

any ones unquestionably would!

Feeling extremely faint, I mustered the last of my strength

to lunge the knife for the middle of his coat!

His coat, which was so tattered and covered…

with layers and layers, of ice and wet snow.

Unfortunately,

my dull little knife could not penetrate that shield, as it should.

*That shield or **KO-JUH** of a coat…*

made from the long hair hide of both sheep and goat,

which was ever so matted, and totally ice entombed.

Thank-God for that protective iced armour!

For, upon a closer look, at his weird hoar-frosted face,

I thought there was something…

something, I may have faintly recognized!

It was those facial features, by heart I should know …

the dark brown eyes, with their twinkling warm glow!

Could this be my spouse?

Was it his eyes that peered at me from underneath those crusty lashes?

Those lashes… so built up by layers and layers, of frozen snow and ice?

Yes, YES!

I praised and thanked-God, rejoicing that he was still alive!

However, walking in that blizzard of a storm…

his life for me,

he shouldn't have placed at such risk and sacrifice!

He wanted to hug me so lovingly, with arms stretched wide…

then immediately halted,

when through the corner of his eye,

THE SATCHEL…he spied.

*Angrily he shouted, "**Shcho to ye?**"*

(What is this,) pointing scornfully to the side.

I had no choice, but to quickly tell all,

for what he saw… was, to some extent right

I had my mindset to take leave of him, and our prized homestead,

if he did not return home from his wanderings,

on that very cold night!

All these new revelations required that my spouse

soothe me with some quick skills of loving-peacekeeping

and thus, this adorable little song he softly sang,

in an endeavour to curtail my bouts,

of such uncontrollable weeping!

It went like this,

OY MO-YE SO-NECH-KO,

NE PLA-CH MO-YE SO-NECH-KO!

YA TUT KO-LO-VAS,

EE TUT BU-DU!

OH MY SUNSHINE,

DON'T CRY MY SUNSHINE!

I'M HERE BESIDE YOU,

AND HERE I'LL STAY!

He wasn't a great singer,

but I'll always remember how superbly he sang that day,

with such passion and sincerity, even now it makes me quiver.

Ah po-teem veen my-ye shlo-zy za-ta-raw

(Later he gently wiped my tears)

Tears, tears, and more tears,

once they commenced, they flowed over like spilt milk.

He then emphatically pronounced, that; no more tears would he allow,

for, there were some extraordinary presents, he wanted me to see.

Next, out of his knapsack, he pulled a pair of warm boots, which by the way…

we were somehow to share, in the coming winter.

Surprisingly, in a separate brown package was something wholly for me!

This securely tied bundle, he handed over,

with one mischievous looking grin and one raised eyebrow.

Tearing open the wrap…a high-fashioned, long,

soft dress unfolded, upon my lap.

It was so intricately woven, made from threads of the finest spun silk!

A dress so beautiful,

so brilliantly highlighted by images of a thousand tiny field flowers,

all painted in a muted, rosy pink!

Instantaneously, my distraught feelings did snap!

This luxurious gift dispelled all thoughts of abandonment

and to each other we gave, a flirtatious quick wink,

settling all misunderstanding!

Donning the well designed, superbly elegant, pink silk dress,

for a tsarina I could have all outsmart,

on her way to a snobbish, high-class imperial ball, had I...

the impressive bejeweled and dazzling, tiara headdress!

Then my charming prince to me did solemnly vow,

never from my side for a moment, would he think to ever part!

This oath, we sealed with one exceptionally long and tight embrace,

then into a stuporous sleep we had fallen, as only exhaustion knows how.

Upon awakening, we both shared an identical reverie so strange...

how in the moonlit night, we stripped the land of every single tree, somehow?

Me, in my silk dress,

and he, elegantly wearing, but only; our new knee-high leather boots!

Hand in hand, we created an entire field so effortlessly,

now waiting for our many calculated plans to chart!

Half-swayed by magical thoughts, that in legendary fables take place,

yet dubious; that overnight, our luck could so absurdly, somehow change!

Our bewilderment needed substantiation ...

so off to the hoar-frosted window we both did race.

To our horror, snow abounded to the bottom of the window frame

and closed off our door, reminding us of the dangers of a winter night's squall.

Yet, such peace followed this growling stormy beast!

The evergreens stood motionless and stately tall,

coated with layers of frost and ice, that shimmered and danced

as far as the eye could possibly see,

displaying a new white coat, from the violent icefall.

Quickly, we knew, this was all a fanciful make believe dream!

But, little did I know at time,

that our pledge or promise "never to part,"

would be so transitory…

and it too, would have such a downer of a theme!

Ale (But,) there are many circumstances in our lives,

whereby we have little or no control,

especially where fate… will next pick-and-roll!

Except; in the end; with each devastating circumstance,

my mind would bend and me cajole…

shifting my thoughts to see more clearly,

the shortness of this life, and life's final goal!

Lives Reunited

Conversing with my Uncle,

I learned that,

my Baba and Grandpa were reunited after a six-month absence,

but an answer to very significant question eluded me

and remained unanswered.

"What brought them together, at that particular time?

Could it maybe have been the works

of something somewhat divine?"

After speaking with my Uncle,

I now know…

this question would have created no confusion for my Baba,

for she somehow knew and could understand,

life as we know it,

was not always up to chance.

But, invariably…

there was a reason for everything,

all governed by God's watchful eye,

and His merciful guiding hand!

My Uncle told me,

on the few times my Baba would now and then regress,

she'd relate to others the strange coincidence…

of the night her spouse returned from the U.S. (United States)

and how their marriage was saved thru His intervention,

along with the wonderful gift…

the gift of the breathtaking, "PINK SILK DRESS!"

Then my Uncle attempted to tell me about his parent's reunion night,

but the voice of my Baba swiftly cut in,

justly; to tell more,

of her own experienced plight.

The night passed much to quickly for me,

well you know what I mean!

With the first visible sign that the sun was about to rise,

off we headed **NA YAR-MA-ROK***,*

(to the market,) in Beausejour…

to spend all our hard earned cash,

on a much-coveted prize!

A team of curly horned oxen strong,

hopeful they'd be somewhat adaptable,

in pulling and tearing up those root stumps…

swelled so unbelievably broad, and long!

Time was pressing to clear away more of our land

and make it ready for spring sowing.

But,

somewhat more imperative

was that our title we needed to maintain,

from possible loss...

due to the known disclaim!

For both man and beast

this was an arduous task

and together we'd all endure,

as yearly…

*the **Go-ver-man IN-SPEC-TOR** would be by to ask.*

"Did you make your ten acres of field this year?"

A question,

we were always afraid to hear!

As homesteaders,

we could lose our land

by a single stroke of a pen,

with no excuses justifiable…

in the opinion of the **In-spec-tor-Man***!*

When this official would make his rounds,

he would pull out a little black book and firmly say…

"Well folks,

if ten acres of field are not plowed…

all rights to the title to be revoked

and off to join the famous skunk man!"

Ha, ha, ha… he so unkindly joked.

For the rules and regulations to uphold your homestead…

are printed in English clear.

That is why the land was resold to the likes of you,

when the previous homesteader,

did not follow the plan.

The plan that is so plainly spelled out…

In This Book Right Here!"

Being made aware of the ill-fate of the skunk man

and this merciless scam,

we became more determined to stave off

or avoid that same exposé!

We stepped up our hours of labour,

struggling with our two stubborn pokey old beasts,

both in the freezing cold of winter

and the dead heat of summer,

from morning to late night,

hollering encouraging words at those oxen till voiceless…

Giddeeup Jake, Giddeeup May;

in the hope of one day creating a magnificent field,

for golden wheat to wave beyond our sight!

It was very hard work…

trying to lay claim to another inch of soil from that dense forest,

leaving hardly any time for personal diversion,

relaxation, or play!

With each sunrise and sunset, I was beginning to fear…

was this all to my life and me being here?"

There seemed to be no end to that task,

of daily stooping over…

pulling and picking at those tree roots and stones,

then dragging them over to the hollowed-out stone boat

with many loud groans!

Tugging

at all those immovable root stumps and gigantic hefty stones,

my body was quickly becoming so gnarled,

and so prematurely old!

I wanted to start a family

and live the life that was meant for me,

as I so longed for the laughter of children

and feet a-pattering, in my own abode!

Ya beel-shy ne ho-tee-la stra-ty-ty mo-ye zyt-ta nad tu ro-bo-tu,

(I no longer wanted to give up my life on that work,)

leaving all of my dreams and aspirations

to be left so unfulfilled,

daily buried under the black furrows of the plow;

while converting the long grass turf into fine particles tilled!

For that field,

I gave up the best years of my life...

repetitively, wiping rolling sweat off my brow,

sprinkling the soil beneath my feet as well as rife,

as a blessing on all future crops it would endow.

Amazingly, the day came when the desires of my heart

were finally heard, and understood...

at which time I was granted, the long awaited role

of sacred Motherhood!

Though I so longed to be blessed by children,

I was beginning to have many a question and many a doubt

as to, how in God's name would I raise them?

Money was scarce! Could we deal with yet another hungry mouth?

Worse was, that my youthful body was beginning to fail me!

My spine and legs chose to bend and bow of their own accord,

limiting my physical activities and capabilities.

I pondered daily, as to the kind of life, this was to be!

Thank God, we had somehow fulfilled the necessary requirements

of the Homestead Act and received our Patent. (Title to the land.)

Tears of Joy, Tears of Silence

There was a heavy lengthy silence…

when neither my Baba, nor my Uncle spoke!

I knew,

that my Baba was childless for an extended period of time,

precisely ten years. Coincidentally,

this happened to be the same amount of time it took to clear all of their land!

It struck me… her body, being so extremely fatigued

was more than likely quite inhospitable to conception

through out that time period!

But, when the task of clearing land was complete…

along came five boys, my dear Dad; Frank,

and Uncles; Stanley, Charlie, Bill and Pete!

She welcomed them dearly,

home birthing… with only a midwife by her feet!

At last she had a daughter, Mary…

so loving, so cherished, so meek,

by my invoking her name, my Uncle suddenly choked up,

and could not a word, further speak.

I could tell by my Uncle's reaction

that this child was the family's most precious delight!

Tragically,

death mercilessly chose her and others,

one grave dark night!

The descended silence then broke, with many a falling tear,

like a menacing cloud that circled and circled,

finally shedding its downpour, with the painful recall of events.

Those events that to my Uncle, were so difficult to volunteer!

"For my sister,

life stopped to early,

but; around the world

such a terrible deadly epidemic was going at that time.

What you go' no do?

There was nothing one could do!

You may not believe this,

but; in my teenage years,

I read the Bible three times over,

all in Ukrainian yet!

I looked for answers to settle my mind.

Because; for the life of me,

I could not understand why?

Why those lives were all taken?

Young people in their prime,

who didn't get to experience life like us!

Boy oh boy, here I'm crying so much, I can't even talk.

Maybe I need to shed a few tears on behalf of my mother,

as somehow, I can't remember if I ever saw or heard her cry.

I do remember she became so sad

and I couldn't think as a child just what to do to comfort her,

beyond giving her an extra hug or two!

Hm-m, I was maybe thirteen, just a kid at the time,

when one upsetting and tragic event was quickly followed by yet another!

Over that flu… she first lost her daughter,

then she heard about the death of her two sisters and her brother.

Quick to follow, was the sad news of her father's passing,

and then some one sent a letter from Ukraine that…

her mother had passed away too!

Such continuous non-relenting grief and sorrow!

Receiving the news of her family's passing,

along with many others perishing from her village,

it was then she dressed herself in black

for the rest of her days, as an expression of her grief!

It is best not to recall this now."

My personal research for this story led me to discover that,

off and on, many people in Ukraine died emaciated from hunger.

This unusual food shortage happened during the years of

1906, 1911, 1921 to 1923,

and the worst food scarcity occurring during the period of

1932 to 1934!

Was this all plausible, to have recurrent failures of harvested crops?

The fertile steppes flowing from the Carpathian Mountains

consistently yielded grain in abundance,

and were better known as the plentiful 'Breadbasket of Europe!'

But it was years later, some fifty-five years after the controlled events

that such devastating and unimaginable news to the world would leak!

Not an Epidemic, not a food shortage, but an induced Great Famine!

A famine of which the world over,

was much too afraid to speak!

For here, evil laughed and danced in one's face...

as a cover-up of all evidence!

Evidence that would bring a lasting shame and disgrace!

To pull off this great deception,

media were paid to alter photos,

as well as to lie and to bluntly write,

how people joyously danced in the streets,

endlessly at all hours, in the day and into the night!

In a mad race to build a Super-Powered Nation,

a tyrannical and brutal plan was induced.

All livestock, as well as produce, that one gathered from the land...

forcefully taken,

along with heirloom treasures

of embroidery and geometrically designed fluffy wool rugs;

to be sent to the head of the Soviet Union on Strictest Command!

All to disable, an inner barter or trade... for a loaf of crusty stale bread,

aiding in a targeted group of people, to be swiftly reduced!

Sworn depositions from eyewitnesses at a Commission of Inquiry*

said…

when hidden grains were all but gone

and hunger needed to be appeased,

some people resorted to boiling hides with weeds

in an attempt to stay alive,

others ate field mice,

frogs, family pets,

or anything else that moved.

It was whispered,

that even cannibalism occurred within families and communities,

and then there were those who took their life,

knowing,

they could no longer thrive.

Some of those found dead on the road way were put aside,

later sold in the open market as "pickled beef in brine,"

a final resting place,

so dishonoured and so undignified!

*First Commission of Inquiry held in 1987, survivors speak of the horrors that occurred during the period of 1932-34, better know as the Great Famine in Ukraine.

Even though vinegar masked the putrid stench of decomposition,

all knew full well what they were eating,

especially when they spotted human digits or toes,

however, the will to stay alive,

 is stronger than… GOD, WHO REALLY KNOWS?

Upon devouring human flesh,

sometimes on the first bite,

death came instantaneously

and did these poor souls smite.

Pleas to other nations of the gruesome scenes

repeatedly happened to fall on,

none other than, so many deaf ears!

Those labelled, as a 'social scum,'

were fated to Self-Extermination,

as for bread they cried.

All told, an estimated seven million or more

Ukrainian peasant people had needlessly died, * 1st.

during this incredibly short period, of some…

one and a half-years!

The grim reality of this "Silent War"

was to quell Ukrainian Nationalism,

by any means…

and speedily encourage amongst the nation's subjects,

a people's new age co-operation!

It came to pass, that…

this appalling task became, mostly complete!

And, in a relatively narrow time span,

friends and family… ceased to exist en masse,

dying an agonizing death from STARVATION!

This superbly well thought out plan and intention…

of promoting Man's Inhumanity To Man;

was shrewdly orchestrated and directed by a ruler,

who attained power by his mighty hand!

And, who acquired a callous satisfaction

in the indulgence of human brutality…

all for a dream or vision,

that **Kol-hosps** *be created, better known as,*

More Collective Land!

Tears of disbelief and gratitude stung the backs my eyes,

as I dwelt on a simple twist of fate!

By coming to Canada,

my Baba's and my Grandpa's lives were spared,

but while here…

many of my Baba's ongoing hardships and sorrows,

she had to learn to deal with on her very own.

For, on and off again,

her so supportive spouse

just happened not to be near,

he was miles and miles away…

as sadness, repeatedly blanketed her heart

and grief, incessantly struck their family home!

He was off in the bush,

where he spent so much of his time…

cutting cordwood to haul to the city,

with the hope of earning an extra nickel or a dime!

And, life for my Baba, moved wearily onward,

without her spouse's embrace of compassion or pity!

I believe, life was a complete struggle for my Baba,

as her son periodically did narrate.

My Baba was mostly left to fend by herself.

She also had the responsibility or charge of…

six growing hungry mouths to feed, clothe, and nurture,

all on her very own, as she found herself repeatedly, home alone!

Then, there were…

the tasks of sewing, cooking, cleaning, canning,

soap making, carding wool, laundry,

as well as the garden, the field,

the livestock, and other chores unknown…

as grinding grain, trapping for fur and meat,

and beekeeping, pursued for candle making and something sweet.

Just recalling my Baba's multiple duties tires me!

There was also an extended period of time,

when her spouse, along with other men

from the bush,

to their home and to their families,

they dared not visit or return.

They had heard that, in the dark of night…

the North-West Mounted Police sought Ukrainians,

hunting them down like criminals, and;

for some unknown reason,

would then take them to some far-off work camps,

*to spend an unlimited time in intern! * 2nd.*

Yes, my Baba must have carried

so many hardships and deep sorrows in her heart!

There were also those heart wrenching final good-byes,

to her two youngest adolescent sons, for evermore.

One lost to a drowning,

the other, who had so willingly signed-up

to bravely fight in the 2nd World War!

A short while later, her young spouse, too;

from the living… did unexpectedly depart.

I learned, while there were many misfortunes that my dear Baba was strewn,

she somehow managed with each taxing situation, to superbly cope…

mostly, by just taking one day at a time, and singing a heartening tune of hope.

Because, in her mind,

liberty required continual strength and courage

in order to proceed…

and, that; neither

discrimination, impoverishment, imprisonment,

nor the blows of death,

were of any reason to be crushed by her personal depression

and allow defeat to concede…

if in this new world,

a better life for her children,

as well as an unshakeable foundation for the future of a nation

were ever to be met!

Footnotes:

1ˢᵗ.

On the east side of the city hall in Winnipeg, Manitoba, Canada - one finds a note-worthy

sculpture of a mother and child carved in granite. This sculpture, was initiated by the Ukrainian

committee and placed on behalf of all Manitoban Ukrainian immigrants who lost family members

and friends to the famine-genocide in Ukraine, or what was then known as the Soviet Union under

communist control. The magnitude of this famine remained concealed from most of the world until

a Commission of Inquiry was held, some fifty years later. Even today, after the Soviets open

admission to the genocide practices; it continues to remain an implausible story to some.

*Next to the aforementioned sculpture is
a bronze plate with the avowed pledge as
printed on the following page*

*Memorial Monument
Sculpted by Roman Kowal*

*Gifted to the city of Winnipeg by
the Ukrainian Canadian Comittee.*

*Unveiled by Mayor Wm. Norrie
on June 24, 1984*

ERECTED TO COMMENORATE THE

50TH ANNIVERSARY

OF THE FAMINE-GENOCIDE IN UKRAINE

1930-33

AND TO THE ETERNAL MEMORY OF OVER 7,000,000

INNOCENT VICTIMS OF FORCED STARVATION: THE

RESULT OF A RUTHLESS PROCUREMENT POLICY

DECREED BY THE SOVIET GOVERNMENT IN MOSCOW.

IN REMEMBRANCE OF THIS TRAGEDY WE STAND

DETERMINED THAT THIS TRAGIC AND INHUMAN ACT SHALL NOT

BE FORGOTTEN, AND THAT SUCH HORRORS SHALL

NEVER BE ALLOWED TO HAPPEN AGAIN.

ON A RENEWED AND BLESSED EARTH
ALL EVIL DEEDS SHALL DISAPPEAR,
AND MOTHERS THERE SHALL BE, AND SONS,
AND TRUTH SHALL REIGN UPON THE EARTH
*TARAS SHEVCHENKO **

DEDICATED THIS 24TH DAY OF JUNE, 1984
UKRAINIAN CANADIAN COMMITTEE,
WINNIPEG BRANCH

Taras Shevchenko *-A renowned Ukrainian artist and poet, more history to follow later.*

Footnotes: *(continued)*

2nd.

*To be interned in one of the Canadian interment camps during the period of 1914 to 1920,
which closely correlated to the time frame of the First World War; an individual had to be
classified as an enemy alien. Strangely, thousands of Ukrainians, along with other Europeans,
were categorized as enemy aliens. Once classified as an enemy alien, these individuals were not
only unjustly imprisoned, but also were forced to do heavy labour in these camps. Across Canada
there were a total of twenty-four of these interment camps. In the province of Manitoba, Brandon
housed one of these internment camps. To the inhabitants, these places of internment were better
known as concentration camps, as those who were held captive within these compounds were
classified as inmates, retained by high wire fences to prevent escapism, and forced to do back
breaking labour in order to obtain a day's food ration. The construction of the Banff National Park
along with many other Canadian National Parks, stand, as a mark forever, of the work carried out
by those enslaved during this period of internment, parks which we take continual pleasure in using,
with little thought as to how they came to be.*

*Many a Ukrainian male was quickly labelled as an enemy alien, especially if he neglected to
obtain his Canadian citizenship papers. Because of a language barrier most individuals did not
understand the importance of filing the necessary paperwork to become a Canadian citizen.
To make matters worse, his passport was usually one of Austria-Hungarian Empire origin.
Immigration authorities and census takers alike often classified these Ukrainian immigrants as
Austrians or Slovaks, and many a time Galician became the designated status quo, especially if they
emigrated from the area known as Galicia, located on the Western side of what is now Ukraine.*

A more humiliating and offensive name that frequently turned up on the intake paperwork of a Ukrainian landed immigrant, was the status of being Rusyn, or Russian. These names all had the most negative connotation to Ukrainians who had so wanted to be recognized for their own ethnic and cultural background and not that of their previous oppressors! But, more importantly, this later name immediately placed them into the alien category because of the significant events that were happening miles across the ocean!

There on the soil that many Ukrainians previously called home, the people were renewing their agitation for an independent Ukraine with the unification of all their lands, controlled either by Austria or Russia; into a single state, along with the overthrow of the tsarist regime, and the abolishment of slavery! This revolt for freedom from oppressors became better known as the 1917 Russian or Bolshevik Revolution! Because of this event, the Ukrainian immigrants in Canada acquired a secondary label, that of having too many revolutionary ideas; and thus they were immediately labelled as high-risk individuals. Suddenly, without just cause, they were seen as being potential big-time troublemakers on this continent!

With the inauguration of the Alien Registration Act, all individuals not holding a valid citizenship papers were to report to a designated headquarters. Upon registering, one soon found that if they were of certain ethic status; they were placed under strict supervision, needing to report weekly to headquarters, others were sent directly to an internment camp. Closely matching the designated profile of an alien caused the sole breadwinner to inevitably lose his job. This invariably left a wife and several children to fend for themselves as the pay to an internee for his labours came to a grand total of twenty-five cents a day. This was hardly enough money to send home to his family when a detainee himself needed to save for replacement socks and boots.

In the city of Winnipeg there were massive job losses as a consequence of the interment and in turn played a major role in the beginnings of the labour strike in Winnipeg on May 15th 1919. With a shortage of labourers, it was an opportune time for city employees to ban together and strike for higher wages! This strike escalated in a shooting and death of a Ukrainian bystander, by the name of Mike Sokolowski on Main Street! His family never claimed his body for burial! It can only be surmised that they feared deportation, as several hundred immigrants were no longer welcome to stay in Canada and were already sent back to their country of origin!

The lowly Ukrainian immigrant who arrived in Manitoba in search of peace, freedom, work, and citizenship was now classified by yet another label, that of "Alien Scum." This label appeared in the Winnipeg Free Press on June 6, 1919 in an advertisement sponsored by the Citizens Committee…

"The problem with this City is the 27,000 Alien Scum living among us,"

This public notice definitely projected the negative attitude that a group of individuals had towards certain new immigrants! The Alien Act, along with this type of newspaper notice, did much to foster a fear in a Ukrainian immigrant! Fearful of being a hunted species, is it any wonder why many Ukrainian males left their spouses and children to head for the forest and stay hidden in the bush! After this indignation, many a Ukrainian had Anglicized their surname in the hope that it would decrease the likelihood of further persecution and allow them equal opportunity at employment!

Part Three

My Baba and I

Remembering Sheds Light

As a young child,

I occasionally saw you, my Baba,

in so much anguish

that in someway I thought I had created,

all while straining to support your frail body;

when to the garden,

you'd ask me to walk you…

just once again.

I've always wondered,

why I had to walk you that long distance,

when only a couple of steps, brought such excruciating pain.

Today, somehow I know…

it was there,

it was there you needed to go,

to check if the cutting blade of the police brigade

destroyed your secret stash,

halting the magical transformation of poppy seeds

into a nutritious sweet bread or roll.

Ah,

there you'd find them still standing,

shielded by the sunflowers and the tall cornrow,

poised and nodding kindly at you,

when the slightest breeze did blow.

It was there!

It was there that you took your many struggles in stride…

amongst your stately poppies,

that gently moved and swayed their fiery red heads nearby,

all appearing to keep time to the melodious music,

your ever-beloved song did provide.

It was there!

It was there you stood with arms outstretched,

with your tired eyes you'd gaze upward onto the sky,

singing loudly…

with the hope of banishing all your sorrows

in your maker,

and reaffirming that…

He would continue to be your guide!

Suddenly,

I'm moved to swiftly glance to my right and to my left,

for I'm roused from my daydream state by

what sounded like a loud gong,

followed by a tune that I've heard numerous times in the garden…

coming at me from a far-off distance,

like the sweetest birdsong!

VA-LY-KEE BOZH, VA-LY-KEE BOZH;

NAD NAS VA-JA-YE,

KOZH-NEE-EE DEN!

VA-LY-KEE BOZH, VA-LY-KEE BOZH;

NAD NAS VA-JA-YE,

KOZH-NEE-EE DEN!

GOD SO BIG, GOD SO BIG;

LOOKS OUT FOR US,

EACH AND EVERY DAY!

GOD SO BIG, GOD SO BIG;

LOOKS OUT FOR US,

EACH AND EVERY DAY!

Reflections of My Baba

As I contemplate the struggles of my Baba's life

and the little that I knew of her,

when as a very young child, in her cozy kitchen I sat,

rocking… back and forth, back and forth,

in her rocking chair so fine,

unexpectedly from no where…

I seem to hear a soft voice like my Baba's, that, in Ukrainian; begins to chat.

"Chy-by ty kho-tee-la po-dee-ly-ty-sa stym khlee-bom znow?"

("Would I like to share some of that bread again?")

Dwelling on her many struggles,

her hardships and her unending pain…

I remain confused, tongue tied, and so unable to speak,

as this incident is somewhat dreamlike, or all somewhat insane!

But, quicker than I could answer…

Yes, Thank-You;

in my most perfect Ukrainian yet,

much like a courteous aristocrat,

there appears a brilliant flash of light, and;

from all danger, I want to hide.

For right there, right before my eyes,

whirling in a sprightly dance is, you know who?

It's my Baba!

Spellbound, my mind and my eyes she does entertain.

By means of her hands, she is motioning from the very start…

with gentle directions, commanding me to follow through,

so I'd have no fear, to run, hide, or become upset!

Her heartening movements captivate the reflective core of my heart

and all those childhood memories of her, I must promptly reset.

For as far back as I can remember…

my Baba was arthritic and old,

always walking slowly, so excruciatingly slow…

Stym pal-kom *(by means of a cane),*

to adjust for life's toils and troubles that had bent her, exceedingly low.

But here she was… a picture of glee!

Such a mesmerizing sight to be seen and to behold!

With what appears to be a bottle drink

and a slices of angelic white bread in hand,

she stands tall, just inches before me!

My heart does flop and skip a beat

and I yearn to embrace this exceptional woman,

this woman so humble, so lowly!

Except, once again,

I'm unable to make the contact I desire

and have to call it a grand defeat!

For I am far too uneasy and apprehensive…

she simply appears so majestic,

so translucent,

and illuminatingly holy!

Could all this be real? Do I have anything to fear?

I want to speak with my Baba,

for there is still so much I'd like to know.

If only I could engage her in a conversation,

to confirm once and for all…

how she managed with her life's great sufferings?

Did she have any regrets when it came to all her sorrow and distress?

These things I wish she'd share with me…

rather than me having to surmise or second-guess!

With a vibrant and glowing smile on her face,

a smile that in my whole life I never did happen to see;

she speedily skirts and dances all about and around me.

Draped in her so familiar mourning attire…

a black skirt and a black top

that cascaded from her neck to her toes,

she gracefully pirouettes,

in felt footwear or **VA-LEEN-KY** up to her knee!

As usual, all her flesh was covered, that on others

normally shows…apart from her hands and face,

which remained, TOTALLY EXPOSED!

There she was, with that long white apron

that once came in handy to remove bread from the oven,

or pick eggs, corn, and many a bean or pea…

along with her unmistakable white kerchief or **BA-BU-SKA**,

covering the small white wisps of hair on her head,

never once to speak of her life and the many hardships she had…

or more precisely, how she managed to live a life of hope,

when through those hard and troubled times, she needed to cope!

But;

it was her calloused and etched arthritic gnarled hands

that spoke so loudly,

they spoke volumes…

of the many years she bore such sacrificial phenomena!

Those overworked hands,

echoed the inscription and the price…

the high price she paid for freedom,

so that her offspring

could live a life of hope!

TO MO-YA U-KRAY-YEEN-SKA BA-BA,

TO MO-YA U-KRAY-YEEN-SKA BA-BA,

VEECH NA-YA PAM-YAT!

MY UKRAINIAN BABA,

MY UKRAINIAN BABA,

ETERNAL MEMORY!

Footnote:

In 1964, my Baba was buried at the Saints Peter and Paul cemetery in Ladywood. Here she lies in eternal rest along with other early pioneers who together toiled the area, many of who were not only her helpful neighbours in life, but also, became her and her spouse's adopted families! Nearby, is her immediate family who predeceased her, children: Mary 1921-1922, Peter 1920-1931, Charlie 1918-1945, and husband Michael 1888-1949.

At this cemetery, some of the older graves lack any type of marker, wooden crosses long rotted, or probably burned by passing prairie fires! Today, these old gravesites are still evident if one looks closely for raised mounds of earth projecting from the flat terrain! In 1999, the community, celebrating 100 years as a parish saw it fitting to mark these unknown gravesites with a simple white metal cross! They also dedicated a cairn in memory of their deceased ancestors, honouring the most significant contribution these people unknowingly made in their lifetime.

When driving north of Beausejour on Highway 12, this cairn can be easily spotted as it is erected close to the roadway. The cairn is made of one impressive white granite rock…a fitting symbol and reminder, of the huge stones our ancestors needed to move, not only to make a field, but also to make a life! The solidness of the stone, appropriately depicts the strength of their personal convictions and integrity that invariably aided them; in the undertaking of the previous mentioned tasks, as well, it so fittingly portrays the foundation on which their daily life principles were based!

On a bronze plaque, this commemorative inscription reads as printed on the following page…

THE ST. PETER & ST. PAUL PARISH

COMMUNITY

REMEMBERS AND HONOURS THE ANCESTORS

WHO NOT ONLY BROUGHT FAITH TO THIS COMMUNITY

SOME 100 YEARS AGO

BUT THROUGH THEIR DAILY EXAMPLE,

SHOWED US THAT WE COULD LIVE IN HARMONY

WITH OUR NEIGHBOURS AND THE WORLD.

THANKS BE TO GOD

DEDICATED JUNE 27,1999

Pictured is the polished limestone rock placed at the Ladywood Saints Peter and Paul Cemetery Ladywood, in honour and remembrance of the early pioneer settlers and ancestors. In my garden, I too, remember my Baba and my roots by planting poppies in and amongst my garden vegetable!

An Angel Conveys a Message

There is eternal life after passing…

both on earth and from the realms above!

For,

such was an angel sent from the heavens,

bearing a story…

that today I know,

unequivocally;

uncovered the invisible strings

of life and love.

A love for a freedom, together with a love for life…

succumbed to a great love of a Neighbour and more so to God,

that when played in harmony,

yielded one of the greatest brilliant symphonies heard on earth!

With an empathetic and helping hand from way above…

this synchronized orchestra reached a crescendo,

when all hopelessness gave way to a new beginning or rebirth;

of faith,

of hope,

and an everlasting, neighbourly love!

With these key ingredients; our immigrant ancestors

effectively overcame the most enduring strife,

by their day-to-day commemorative…

in the Breaking and the Sharing… of the Bread and Salt of Life!

Many thoughts swarm my mind

as I sit and into far outer space just stare…

only to be interrupted and enraptured

by the voice of my Baba, coming at me loud and clear;

from off in a great distance somewhere,

even birds stopped to listen,

silencing their chirping and triumphant hoopla.

"Oh by the way, there's something you ought to know… We,

who packed up our meager belongings and bravely answered 'The Call,'

gave up our motherland and previous life…

to journey to a place known as Canada! Not as opportunists,

with the hope we'd strike it rich in a wealth of silver or gold!

but, in search of a new freedom, or a vision…

for future generations to unfold!

Embarking on this new life, there were many inner pangs of guilt.

Those so attacked our minds, and were difficult to subdue,

for hastily abandoning our troubled homelands in such despair;

along with all our new trials and tribulations

which inevitably would daily ensue,

left us wholly unaware of the lasting impact

that today, many declare…

were the stones that built up this Great Nation.

A nation they say, the world-over, looks up to!

Being new immigrants in a strange land,

there were a lot of unknowns with which to cope.

But, through mutual respect and tolerance,

love transcended all barriers between neighbours,

permitting us to triumph over our diversities

as well as our worse adversities and strife…

because, each of us had the power and the capacity within us,

to embrace life, with love, and hope;

when from the chains of oppression we finally broke

and so courageously, we did elope.

Yes we came here, so that you can experience life!"

Hearing this message from my Baba was a changing moment for me.

For the very first time in my life; the blindness…

that totally obliterated so many things since childhood,

allowed my eyes to be opened to see.

I had long ago, deduced that…

the heroic sacrifices that were made by my ancestors and yours,

were made to benefit all,

but at this moment, they mostly benefited me!

Thru personal reflection I came to realize,

that the strings of life and hope are within human grasp!

It became so clear, when I allowed myself to step back…

into the lives of my pioneer ancestors

and there momentarily, their life to clasp.

All was self-evident, at last!

We will undoubtedly, forever remain…

tied to the strings of our ancestors past,

simply because of their amazing, untold legacy!

That being…their enduring quest for freedom

for their children and grandchildren!

It is for this humble reason,

we must not EVER relinquish their lead,

of putting aside our differences

and helping those, who are in a much more desperate need!

As there are millions in this world that daily endure hunger and poverty

and millions more who are terrorized and suffer,

the tortures of the dammed under oppressive hands

and long for…

"That," which we can so freely give…

our voices persistently and unrelentingly loud and strong,

to promote peace and reconciliation in the far-off lands…

Lands,

where our immigrant roots and origins had at one time sprung,

along with the sharing of bread to promote life,

so that, not only you and I, but all of humanity may truly live,

endorsing integrity to multiply

and subtly cleansing the world…

of all discord,

war, and strife!

The torch, which was once placed into our ancestors' hands,

is placed into the hands

of each and every successive generation that follows,

to continue the metamorphosis of individual hearts,

for we are all connected!

Connected to the same mystical story,

as through life each of us wallows...

given that, the only God-given gifts for anyone's future are,

Love and Hope!

The tools necessary to bring about what everyone so infinitely desires,

that being freedom, justice, and true peace,

to come into our world scope!

Thus, if we carry on with their journey,

doing our part...

sharing "That," which makes us Canadians,

surely, we will not then negate our ancestor's heart!

For, the freedom which they sought…

was far from being free,

and; as a payment for their sacrifices,

we must guard against… all future inequity.

From their examples

we must not falter …

nor from their footsteps stray,

always living for our neighbours,

till the whole world around us

sees the same light of day.

Ultimately,

by working and building together,

we will all one day jubilantly sing and dance…

for these were the gifts

our immigrant ancestors left behind,

Gifts To Share,

Gifts Of My…

And,

I Do Believe,

YOUR INHERITANCE!

My Bandura's Enduring Spirit

You are nothing but boards that I put together with glue

while to some people in this world you are their soul…

Today, you've come to be

a nation's national symbol,

portraying an immense struggle towards freedom and autonomy!

Once, in the not so distant past,

you were put to death during a communist regime.

Your strings were all cut,

your body destroyed,

leaving the performer distraught and aghast!

For those who harmonized with you,

singing loudly for freedom…

saw a long-term jail sentence,

most times, a quick death by a sharp shooting firing squad!

BUT YOU DID NOT DIE!

As I carved and sanded your frame,

your unwavering spirit came to life…

settling deep into my soul

and for my undivided attention you would daily vie!

In you, I heard the finest assortment of music, from soft and melodious

to loud and thunderous, even though you lacked every one of your strings!

Your music found me wanting to visit and dance with my Baba,

as it uncovered and revealed melodies and memories of my childhood and hers,

incredibly; somehow…

all were brought to life from the past!

Your music, amazingly took me to the awesome country,

which my Baba had left behind, so long, long ago… in her search of a new terrain.

Sometimes, your music was terribly haunting!

Oddly, it too was reassuring,

as it retold of her life's many hardships and her ability to deal with…

life's ongoing trials and pain!

But, your music became more joyful and more carefree,

when it resounded of how fate had spared her from repression…

by the newfound freedom she had obtained.

Your music continues to play a melody,

which resounds from every corner of our world, up surging with each gust of wind!

Repeatedly it plays the same message…

to stand up in solidarity and support of that same freedom for others,

so that their journey to liberty and independence… could also be attained!

A Bandurist's Song

VAZ-OW SO-BEE BAN-DU-RU…TYE ZA-HRAW SHCHO ZNAW.

VAZ-OW SO-BEE BAN-DU-RU…TYE ZA-HRAW SHCHO ZNAW.

CHA-REZ TU BAN-DU-RU…BAN-DU-RE-STOM STAW!

CHA-REZ TU BAN-DU-RU… KOB-ZA-RE-STOM STAW!

Took myself a Bandura and played what I knew.

Took myself a Bandura and played what I knew.

Over that Bandura a bandurist I became!

Over that Bandura a kobzar I became!

This song brings me back to the very beginning of this story. It appears that those who allow themselves to pick up a bandura are magically capable of becoming a Bandurist, or a Kobzar, the latter if the instrument is used to tell a story!

The masculine pronoun has been left unaltered in this traditional Ukrainian melody as it was only men that sang this song in the past, not just any men, but men made blind by war! Learning to play this multi-stringed instrument, while blind, aided these individuals to beg for bread or alms more discreetly; all with the unfailing hope of lessening their level of poverty!

On the east side of the Manitoba Legislative grounds, in the city of Winnipeg this stately figure of Taras Shevchenko sits as a Memorial Monument. Note, the Bandurist (center most) depicted on the perimeter base.

Designed by Andry Daragan, Modern Art Foundry, New York, N.Y. U.S.A.

Du-my Mo-yee, Du-my Mo-yee

(MY THOUGHTS, MY THOUGHTS,)

WITH THEM

THERE IS SADNESS!

WHAT WAS THE REASON

THAT YOU ON PAPER STOPPED

WOEFUL LINE UPON LINE?

WHY DID THE WINDS NOT UNFURL YOU

UPON THE STEPPES,

LIKE DUST?

WHY DOES MY SADNESS

NOT OVERSLEEP,

LIKE MY OWN YOUNG CHILDREN?

As my book draws near to completion, the sentiment of this verse is one that haunted me as my thoughts were put on paper. The renowned poet, Taras Shevchenko wrote the above poem in 1839 in St. Petersburg. I attempted to translate his poem for you the reader, from Ukrainian into English, after attending only a few Ukrainian language classes! The translation may not be one hundred percent accurate, simply because I am still a novice, and the fact that certain words cannot be translated easily into another language!

History of Author – *Taras Shevchenko (1814-61) was born in the region known as Ukraine. He was of peasant lineage and thus doomed to a life of serfdom and suppression, given that, at the time of his birth and youth, his country was under the Tsarist Rule of Russia. Orphaned as a teenager, his confidant and friend became his thoughts and his sketchpad. On the later, he sketched many a picture or wrote many a poem for which he later became renowned. One of his earliest writings, entitled Kobzar or The Bard, included an eloquent collection of eight romanticized poems based on historical themes, all of which echoed his love for his country and its people.*

To the inhabitants of Ukraine, Taras Shevchenko's paintings, together with his lyrical writings, quickly made him legendary, in the field of art. Most of his written poetry was adapted to music and performed by many a Kobzar minstrel, thus legends, folklore, as well as Ukrainian history, were kept well alive with the passage of time.

When he was a more mature adult; his later writings, dealt mostly with the social injustices and the oppression of not only the downtrodden people of his own country but also the world over. More than a century and a half ago, he stirred national consciousness with his undeniable passion to elevate the poor from their struggles, to one of hope; through his revolutionary writings and solutions to the many injustices taking place in his society!

Taras Shevchenko's poetic expressions, with his enduring hope of seeing a justice prevail for all subjugated humanity; have left a mark on the whole of society! His insightful messages advocating social justice for all, have been translated into several different languages and have overtime influenced many an author, myself included.

We Too Can Make a Difference

As a third generation Canadian, life for me is good, but my 'being' within this nation, I at times, indisputably, take for granted, as probably do most Canadians. In my moments of gratitude, I come up short for right words in either English or Ukrainian, to express my thankfulness for the opportunities, the freedoms, and life's abundance that we as a nation have gained, all as a result of the sacrifices made by our multi-lingual and colourful ancestors of our past!

As beneficiaries of the sacrifices made by others, I believe that together, we too can make a difference in the lives of others! Thus, all net profits from the sale of this story, and / or live presentations, as well as readings are in support of hungry young children in Ukraine. Today, many children in that country continue to suffer from the effects of a long-term economic instability. An instability that over time was created as a consequence of ravaging wars and dominance, which happened to so plague these peoples for the last 500 years!

With the collapse of communism in 1991, Ukraine won it's Independence, and the people, at last; were released from the chains of oppression, but the chains of hunger have not released the children for play. In the year 2000, on my visit to Ukraine, it was not uncommon to see very young children alone on the streets, with their small-outstretched hand, begging, for none other than Bread…with an old familiar chant!

DA-YE-TE ME-NEE HLEEB, DA-YE-TE ME-NEE HLEEB,
DA-YE-TE ME-NEE HLEEB, SHCHO-BY BOH VAM-PO-MA-HAW!
GIVE ME BREAD, GIVE ME BREAD,
GIVE ME BREAD, SO THAT GOD WILL HELP YOU!

Given that, begging does not always get food into the mouths of the hungry, a new development is taking place in Ukraine. Because this country is still coping with the dynamics of its newly acquired independence, it has yet to establish some form of aid to low income families.

Parents, experiencing socio-economic problems and in need of aid, are choosing to place their children into orphanages, all with the hope that their offspring would have a better chance of survival to adulthood! Statistically, this alarming trend has some one hundred thousand children reportedly living within these institutions in the year 2004.

If you desire further information in prearranging a live presentation, or reading; in support of making a change in the fate of these children's lives, from one of hopelessness to one of hope, please contact me by E-mail at the address below.

Liz
ttebchorney@hotmail.com

This land is your land
this land is my land,
including the oceans
and all the islands!
One should not hunger,
within this bounty,
this world of plenty,
that was made for you and me!
This land, was made…
for all to be!

Epilogue

In the year 2000, I did visit the homeland of my grandparents' birth. There, my childhood inhibition to speak Ukrainian had surprisingly vanished, especially when primed with fiery vodka. Incidentally, upon my arrival home, I did enroll into more formal Ukrainian classes as a mature student, now that I was no longer fearful of my language, my roots, or my culture betraying me, and I knew, that; I could handle those who made me feel less of a Canadian!

While in Ukraine, I saw the castle-like monastery where my Baba had once worked! Sadly, many a small enterprise that built the Bandura instrument had its demise during the communist regime, along with the demise or annihilation of poets, writers, dramatists, novelist, composers, humorists, Bandurists and Kobzars!

As was mentioned, under the communist rule, the telling of a story through song, along with the help of the musical strings of a Bandura, was totally banned! This activity was oddly labelled as, "counterrevolutionary", and, one would pay dearly, if the ban were ignored. For those who disregarded this ban, their instruments were destroyed in some fashion, i.e. strings cut, or the instrument were smashed completely, and a long-term jail sentence or death by the firing squad awaited the artist! In an open market, hanging from a rope on a roof rafter, my eyes spotted a Bandura that appeared somewhat like mine… that is, lacking all its strings! I couldn't help but wonder of the history and the fate of that forlorn looking Bandura suspended in mid-air by a cord tied to its neck base! Could it have been made unplayable because it was forcefully silenced?

Today, my bandura continues to wait for its strings. In the interim, I luckily found another one, locally, with more strings attached than I bargained for… that I tell this story. Not only tell this story, but also encourage others to do the same!

With that said, go on, recall the roots of your ancestors and write those memories down, as there are many more stories to be told of our culture and heritage, all of which make up our shared diverse history as a nation. When you've compiled your stories become ambassadors of this information! Tell them to all who will listen, and sing like you don't need the money, for we have much to celebrate, as we too, "are a called people," for whom a plan is destined, if only we listen to, 'That Voice.' A voice, which daily encourages all to break and share the greatest gift bestowed upon us, the gift of our inherent humanity… that is to share the bread and salt of life, so bequeathed to us by our ancestors!

The writing of this story has made me recognize, what my ancestors sought is no different from what I seek, two generations later; this being… peace, security, and basic provisions for my children and all children of the world, in this generation and other generations to follow! I also realized that I am a part of something bigger, and that, my hopes and dreams for tomorrow will always remain intertwined and strongly bound, all to stay tangled in the strings of my ancestral past! For there, the fruits of their wisdom were lying dormant along the pathway of life, just waiting to be found… left at hand to harvest and too broadcast!

I feel, we as a nation, must continue on the path where our enlightened ancestors left off, sharing our time and resources with others, welcoming and appreciating what each new immigrant has to offer, but more importantly, standing up and saying a loud 'no' to racism, prejudice, and hate in all its guises and disguises! Each of us in our own way, needs to ensure we remain, the Canada, which those before us struggled and fought to establish!

We are a country, which now has its own Charter of Human Rights and Freedoms. Something that other nations only can hope to aspire to and look to us to lead them on. Nations, which we as Canadians could easily help, to attain their own autonomy and independence!

Because of our present world crisis of mayhem and madness, we can no longer remain immobilized through apathy, or sit idly by, with the hope that our political leaders will do us right. We as a people must become mobilized, as there are many in need of our aid either because of natural disasters or those created by man. Many problems continue to exist for a lot of inhabitants of different nations in this world. People suffering from poor nutrition, lack of proper shelter, education and health, all due to the lack of resources, working capital, corruption and present or past wars!

If we as Canadians stepped our efforts in responsibility and action, spreading that same benevolence and compassion that we learned from our ancestors, and by extending it to all other world communities, maybe then, peace and harmony will become a possibility for all! For, the sharing and goodwill that supported our ancestors to not only survive, also aided them as a nation's people to become more tolerant and aware of the needs of others... this continues to follow and mark us to this day as to what it is, to be truly Canadian.

United as one, we too can leave an incredible communal sign, a sign of hopefulness for this generation and others to emulate! Yes, so overwhelmingly immeasurable are the gifts our ancestors left us regarding the lessons of this celebrated life, our immigrant ancestors, many, of whom knew neither, how to read, nor how to write!

Printed in the United States
by Baker & Taylor Publisher Services